101 Inclusive
& SEN Humanities
& Language
Lessons

101 Inclusive

& SEN Humanities

& Language

Lessons

FUN ACTIVITIES & LESSON PLANS

for Children Aged 3–11

Kate Bradley and Claire Brewer

Jessica Kingsley *Publishers*
London and Philadelphia

First published in 2019
by Jessica Kingsley Publishers
73 Collier Street
London N1 9BE, UK
and
400 Market Street, Suite 400
Philadelphia, PA 19106, USA

www.jkp.com

Copyright © Kate Bradley and Claire Brewer 2019

Front cover image source: Kara McHale.

Library of Congress Cataloging in Publication Data
Names: Bradley, Kate (Kathryn D.), author. | Brewer, Claire, author.
Title: 101 inclusive and SEN humanities and language lessons : fun activities and lesson plans for children aged 3-11 / Kate Bradley and Claire Brewer.
Other titles: One hundred and one inclusive and SEN humanities and language lessons
Description: London ; Philadelphia : Jessica Kingsley Publishers, 2019.
Identifiers: LCCN 2018020640 | ISBN 9781785923678
Subjects: LCSH: Humanities--Study and teaching (Elementary)--Activity programs. | Geography--Study and teaching (Elementary)--Activity programs. | History--Study and teaching (Elementary)--Activity programs. | Language and languages--Study and teaching (Elementary)--Activity programs. | Special education--Activity programs. | Inclusive education.
Classification: LCC LC1011 .B67 2019 | DDC 372.8--dc23 LC record available at https://lccn.loc.gov/2018020640

British Library Cataloguing in Publication Data
A CIP catalogue record for this book is available from the British Library

ISBN 978 1 78592 367 8
eISBN 978 1 78450 710 7

Printed and bound by CPI Group (UK) Ltd, Croydon, CR0 4YY

Contents

Introduction. 9

STARTERS

Past and Present Snap. 14
Shop for It 15
Old House, New House. 16
Above the Land 17
Under the Sea. 18
Where Do I Belong?. 19
Mountain, River, Tree, Stone 20
Canard, Canard, Oie! 21
Musical Statues 22
Colour Sort 23

GEOGRAPHY

EMERGING
1. Sensory Box Fire Station 26
2. Seaside Exploration. 27
3. Whatever Is the Weather? 28
4. Nee-Nah Nee-Nah 29
5. The Shop. 30
6. Room Hunt. 31
7. Move Me. 33
8. Find Me Fetch Me Dress Me 34
9. In the Woods or in the Town? 35
10. Where I Truly Belong 37
11. Wish You Were Here! 38
12. Where Do I Work? 39
13. Autumn Leaf Walk 41
14. Leaf Snap 42

DEVELOPING

15. Natural or Made? 43
16. Who Made It? 44
17. I Went to the Shop and I Bought.... 45
18. Where Shall I Sit?. 46
19. Today, I Am... 47
20. Over Here or There? 48
21. Build-a-Town. 49
22. My Choice .50
23. Playground Planning 51
24. Recycle Me Do 52
25. All Help Together. 53
26. Follow the Arrows 54

SECURING

27. Roll-a-Feature 55
28. Mark It Down 56
29. Who Am I? .57
30. It's a Wide Wide World 58
31. Take Me There 59
32. Land, Air and Sea 60
33. This Is Pretty 61

HISTORY

EMERGING

34. Here I Am! .64
35. It's Me! 65
36. Summer or Winter? 66
37. Days of the Week 67
38. Feely Bag Routine 68
39. That's Old .69
40. Assembly Remembering 70
41. This One Time 71
42. Adult or Baby? 72
43. How Rome Was Built 73
44. How We Travelled 74
45. No Plastic Here 75

DEVELOPING

46. Victorian Me 76
47. Play That Video 77
48. Me: Past and Now 78
49. History Dig 79
50. Vroom 81
51. Guess Who! 82
52. From Baby to Now 84
53. Who Plays with This? 85
54. Let Down Your Hair! 87

SECURING

55. Through the Tunnel 88
56. Let's Play! 90
57. Today or Yesterday? 91
58. My Week 93
59. Weekend Tales 94
60. Sherlock 95
61. On Stage 97

LANGUAGES

EMERGING

62. Drum Circle 100
63. Sing It Differently 101
64. Me for My Turn! 102
65. Simon Dit… 103
66. Action Me! 104
67. Play It with Me 105
68. Colour Hunt 106
69. Hello, Bonjour, Ciao 108
70. Stop! Go! 109
71. Teddy Wants… 110
72. Good, Bad, OK 111
73. Roll It, Move It 112

DEVELOPING

74. Ola! 113
75. Language Whispers 114

76. Rojo, Naranja, Verde 115
77. I Want… 116
78. Tasty Talking 117
79. Do You Like Spinach Ice Cream? 118
80. Action Match!. 119
81. See It, Find It 120
82. Release Me!. 121
83. Are You at School Today?. 122
84. aMAZEing Directions. 123
85. Translate Me 124
86. Numeral Naming 126
87. Story Time 127

SECURING

88. Sensational Story Telling 128
89. Bingo! 129
90. Roll-a-Command 130
91. Big Art 131
92. Colour Race 132
93. Old MacDonald. 133
94. Numero Beetle 134
95. Shake Shake Shake! 135
96. Fruit Tally. 136
97. Classroom Calamity. 137
98. Name That Animal 138
99. On a Picnic 139
100. Fruit Shop 140
101. Wacky Racing 141

Introduction

Hello and welcome to the fourth book in our '101 Inclusive and SEN Lessons' series!

While changes to school funding are affecting the way schools are able to support complex learners in classrooms, we remain passionate about ensuring children with special educational needs (SEN) receive a broad, balanced, creative and accessible curriculum. With this book full of practical and exciting lessons we hope to support teachers, teaching assistants, parents and other professionals to include all children in their planning and teaching across an increasing range of curriculum subjects.

With the government accepting the recommendations of the Rochford Review and P Levels no longer being a statutory assessment for children working below national curriculum levels from September 2018,[1] we understand that many schools and practitioners may find that there are currently few options to replace them. Thus, we feel that P Levels still offer an invaluable approach to structuring lessons and progression for children with SEN. The lessons in this book are still designed to meet the objectives set out in the P Level document.[2] However, these are simply a guideline to direct adults working with complex learners to choose lessons that are appropriate to the child's current level of understanding and development.

Each chapter starts with objectives designed for the most complex learners and works up towards more challenging objectives. Plenaries have been included for each lesson in order to provide an obvious end point for the child. We have included ideas for ways to consolidate learning as, for children with SEN, doing an activity once is unlikely to support their understanding of a concept.

---

1   Standards and Testing Agency (2016) *Rochford Review: Final Report*. London: DfE.
2   Department for Education & Standards and Testing Agency (2017) *Performance (P Scale) Attainment Targets for Pupils with Special Educational Needs*. London: DfE.

The book also includes a chapter of starters designed to engage children in motivating learning styles from the beginning of each lesson. It is up to you to decide which starters suit which lesson you are teaching, as you may want to meet a range of additional skills in one session.

Humanities and Languages may not automatically be topics that you see as priorities for children with complex learning needs, yet when you start looking at the objectives you quickly realise that the focus is on understanding themselves and their world better. Languages are not typically taught until KS2 (around 7–8 years old) in English schools, and so whilst you could start earlier if you felt it appropriate, we have planned the languages lessons with a slightly older child in mind.

We have both used many of these ideas in our classrooms and wider practice and hope that you enjoy teaching with them in yours!

Kate and Claire

Follow and share your ideas with us: @Kate_Brads, @clairebrewers

What Do We Mean by Additional Skills?

- Kinaesthetic: movement is important to stimulate the child and provide learning experiences that do not revolve around sitting at a table and chair.

- Auditory: being able to develop listening and processing skills in a variety of subjects across the school day will support children to become more attentive in lessons and life.

- Fine motor: these are the skills that involve doing activities on a smaller scale. Developing these skills supports handwriting, dressing and manipulation in the long term.

- Gross motor: these involve the big muscle groups in the body and are large-scale movements. Developing these skills supports trunk control, coordination and motor planning.

- Tactile: skin covers the entirety of the body and is the largest sensory system. Having difficulties processing tactile input (such as getting messy) means that the children don't explore and experience the world to its full potential.

- Attention: a child's ability to attain and engage in activities to their full extent needs time and patience. The ability to focus on an individual activity for a longer period of time enables learning to take place. By providing exciting, short activities you can build a child's tolerance to this.

- Communication: with reference to communication, this is about receptive (listening to) and expressive (responding to) language. Language does not have to be speech; this can be in the form of visuals, switches and gesture.

- Social communication: this is about the vital skills of sharing time and experience with a partner, turn taking and knowing rules within social situations and games.

Resources

This is not an exhaustive list but, where possible, we have used resources that we find easily in our own classrooms, so that life is not made harder for you by having to go out of your way to prepare extra resources for the lessons.

Resources that you will use throughout the book:

- builder's tray

- choosing board (large firm board with strips of Velcro to attach symbols and pictures)

- laminating sheets and access to a laminator

- water and sand tray

- messy media e.g. flour, cornflour, shaving foam/play foam

- small world characters (especially for 'people who help us')

- cars

- trains

- whiteboard and pens

- chalk

- felt-tip pens

- pencils
- electronic tablet
- sensory toys (flashing balls, massage cream, hand massagers)
- canvas bag
- tidy-up box
- scissors
- teddy bears and dolls
- boxes
- dressing up items
- mirrors
- large pocket dice
- access to historical artefacts relevant to the topic e.g. the Romans, old and new toys
- Internet access
- cameras
- interactive whiteboard
- beebots
- communication switches

STARTERS

Past and Present Snap

RESOURCES

Laminated cards (two x same image of range of modern and old household items)

ACTIVITY

- Deal the cards to all the people who are playing.

- First person places a card face up in the centre of the table.

- This repeats around the group.

- As two cards match, the first person to say 'snap' wins that pair of cards.

- Repeat.

- If the cards run out, reshuffle and deal.

- The winner is the one with the most pairs.

Teaching note: to make this more challenging, create a pack of cards that have one old and new item and the children have to match the two.

Shop for It

RESOURCES

List for each player with the items that are on the cards

Laminated square cards of a range of household items

ACTIVITY

- Give each player a shopping list.

- Place all the cards face down in the centre of the table.

- Each player looks at their shopping list and works out what they need to look for.

- Taking turns, turn a card over. If you need it, you keep it; if you do not, it goes back in the same place.

- Repeat until one player has found all the items on their list.

Old House, New House

RESOURCES

Dolls house items that you would find in each house, or pictures if items not available

Large pictures of the inside of a Victorian house and a modern house (at least A3)

ACTIVITY

- Place all of the items (or pictures) in a box. Present the two pictures of the houses to the group.

- Talk about what they notice. Which house would they like to live in?

- Open the box and allow each person to take out an item (or picture): which house would it go in?

- Repeat until all the items have been placed in the houses.

Above the Land

RESOURCES

Chairs

Access to large screen and Internet

'Tickets'

Fan or cardboard

ACTIVITY

- Place the chairs in pairs with an aisle between them (an aeroplane set up) in front of the screen.

- On the screen have a video ready of boarding an aeroplane, an aeroplane taking off, flying through the clouds and landing.

- As the children enter the room, give each a ticket and play the boarding video. Encourage the children to find a chair and show their ticket to the adults.

- Then play the take-off video and use the fan (or cardboard) to blow wind on the children.

- Change the video to flying through the clouds: what shapes can they see?

- Finish with the plane landing and the children getting off.

Teaching note: you can add as many props to this starter as you like. Luggage, seat numbers, snacks, voice announcements would all work well.

Under the Sea

RESOURCES

Goggles

Access to screen and Internet

Parachute

Water spray bottles

ACTIVITY

- Give each child a pair of goggles before they enter the space; have a video of under the sea playing on the screen.

- Waft the parachute above the children's heads; encourage them to make swimming type movements.

- Spray the children lightly with water from the spray bottles.

Teaching note: you can add many more props to this. A boat, treasure, fish and flippers would all be good additions.

Where Do I Belong?

RESOURCES

Canvas bag

Real items that represent land, air and sea e.g. shells, feathers, stones, seaweed, grass, fish, sticks, leaves

Pictures of land, air and sea

ACTIVITY

- Place the real items in the canvas bag.

- Place the three pictures of land, air and sea in front of the group.

- Ask a child to put their hand in the bag and find an item. Ask them to take a guess before they pull it out.

- When they have guessed and looked at it, ask them where it belongs. Do the rest of the group agree?

Teaching note: some of the items may belong in two places, which is OK. Encourage the children to talk about the differences and come to a decision about which is the best picture for it to go on.

Mountain, River, Tree, Stone

RESOURCES

Visuals of a mountain, river, stone and a tree on separate cards

ACTIVITY

Each of the items has an associated action, so before the game, teach the children these actions: for a mountain they need to stand still with their arms in a point above their head; for a tree they need to put their arms out to the side and float them around; for the river they need to lie on the floor and wiggle; finally, for the stone, they need to curl into a ball.

Say one of the features and show the card and the children all do the action.

Have a few practice turns.

Once the game starts, the last one to get in position is out.

Repeat until there is a winner.

Teaching note: once the children get used to the game, they can be the ones who hold the cards and call out the action words.

Canard, Canard, Oie!

RESOURCES

None

ACTIVITY

- Sit the children in a circle; adults can join in too.

- Model to the children playing 'duck, duck, goose' using the target language names.

- Child who is 'it' goes around the outside of the circle saying 'duck, duck, duck, duck'; when the child says 'goose!' the goose runs around the circle after the child.

- The goose is then 'it' and becomes the person walking around the circle.

Musical Statues

RESOURCES

Songs in the target language

Access to music player and speakers

ACTIVITY

- Move the furniture out of the way so that everyone has space to dance.

- Play a song in the target language and encourage everyone to dance.

- When the music stops, shout 'freeze' and encourage all the children to freeze.

- Anyone who does not is out.

- Continue playing a range of songs.

Colour Sort

RESOURCES

Ribbons or streamers in a range of colours

Images of each colour with the name of the colour written in the target language below

ACTIVITY

- Gather all of the children in the centre of the room.

- Show them each of the images with the colour and say the name of the colour in the target language; ask the children to repeat.

- Place the images around the room.

- Hold the bag of ribbons or streamers and say 'Ready, steady, drop!'; empty the contents on the floor.

- Start the timer and encourage the children to take one streamer or ribbon at a time and place it next to the image of the matching colour.

- When everything is sorted, using the target language, ask the child to collect the 'red' items and so on.

GEOGRAPHY

1. Sensory Box Fire Station

Learning Objective

Emerging

Pupils extend the skills they need to help them explore the world.

Additional Skills

Tactile: experiencing different textures.

Gross and fine motor: handling and placing different sized objects.

Social communication: taking part in a play activity.

Resources

2–3 transparent plastic boxes

A range of sensory media e.g. oats, rice, cereal, flour, damp sand, shaving foam (see Teaching note for advice)

A range of items and toys associated with the fire station e.g. small world firefighter figures, firefighter hat, uniform, fire engine, pretend fire hose, etc.

An area in the classroom or outside to set up fire station role play

MAIN

- To set up this activity fill each transparent plastic box with a different sensory media and hide the range of items and toys associated with the fire station in the sensory boxes. Place the boxes in the area where the fire station role play can be set up.

- Support the children to come over to the sensory boxes and to search in the boxes for the hidden items and toys.

- Each time the children find an item, verbally label it for them and support them to place it in the role play area.

- Continue until all the items have been found and placed in the role play area.

PLENARY

Once all the items and toys have been found, support the children to explore and play with them. Adult can model role play e.g. putting on hat and using hose to put out pretend fire.

CONSOLIDATION ACTIVITIES

Set this activity up again but use different items and toys associated with 'people who help us' scenarios e.g. post office, police station, hospital.

Teaching note: some children can find exploring sensory media challenging so choose the type of media that is put in the boxes carefully by referring to a messy play texture hierarchy.

2. Seaside Exploration

Learning Objective

Emerging

Pupils handle artefacts and materials given to them.

Additional Skills

Gross and fine motor: handling and placing different sized objects.

Attention: able to sustain concentration on an adult-led activity for 5 minutes.

Tactile: exploring and experiencing different textures.

Resources

Builder's tray

A range of natural artefacts and materials found at the seaside e.g. shells, fossils, pebbles, salted water in a jug, sand, seaweed

A range of human made artefacts and materials found at the seaside e.g. bucket and spade, lollipop sticks, swimming trunks, boats

Two boxes for the natural and human made resources

MAIN

- Support the children to come over to the builder's tray.

- Explain that we are going to explore the seaside!

- Hand the children each natural artefact and material found at the seaside. Verbally label the object and encourage the children to handle and explore it before placing in the builder's tray.

- Repeat this for the human made resources until all the artefacts and materials are placed in the builder's tray.

- Support the children to look in the builder's tray and use language such as 'Look, the pebbles are wet in the water.'

PLENARY

Once all the artefacts and materials are placed in the builder's tray support the children to handle them by exploring and playing with the items in a way appropriate to the seaside e.g. filling the bucket with sand, plopping pebbles in the water. Label the items the children are handling and if they are natural or human made.

CONSOLIDATION ACTIVITIES

Whenever introducing a new topic in Geography support the children to explore the new materials and artefacts associated with the topic in the same way e.g. if learning about rivers support the children to handle natural and human made objects associated with rivers and make a river scenario in the builder's tray to explore.

3. Whatever Is the Weather?

Learning Objective

Emerging

Pupils know that certain actions produce predictable results.

Additional Skills

Communication: indicating a choice to a familiar adult.

Gross motor: using a flat hand to operate a communication switch.

Attention: able to sustain concentration on an adult-led activity for 5 minutes.

Resources

Communication switches pre-recorded with the words 'rain', 'wind', 'snow' and 'sun'

Symbols for 'rain', 'wind', 'snow' and 'sun' on top of each communication switch

Water spray

Shaving foam

Handheld or battery fan

Sunglasses

MAIN

- Support each child to sit opposite the adult.

- Adult sings the following to the tune of 'Farmer's in the Den': 'Whatever is the weather? Whatever is the weather? Oh my, oh my, whatever is the weather?'

- Then present the child with the communication switches and support the child to press a switch.

- If the communication switch says 'rain' spray the child with the water spray; if 'snow' clap a small blob of shaving foam over the child; if 'wind' fan the child with fan; if 'sun' give the child the sunglasses to explore.

- Repeat the song, give the child the choice of switches again, and respond to their choice each time.

PLENARY

With the child go to a window and look out at the weather for that day. Sing the song with the child and use the appropriate communication switch and prop for that particular day. Make it clear to the child that e.g. 'Today the weather is windy!'

CONSOLIDATION ACTIVITIES

When the child is exploring outside take out the appropriate communication switch and prop for the weather that day. Sing the song with the child; support them to press the switch and then to explore the prop. If the child is able, support them to present the switch to a classmate and then to use the prop with their friend.

Teaching note: when introducing this activity to the child start with just two communication switches and slowly introduce more switches so that the choice the child makes is meaningful.

4. Nee-Nah Nee-Nah

Learning Objective

Emerging

Pupils know that certain actions produce predictable results.

Additional Skills

Visual: matching pictures to objects.

Auditory: noticing a sound.

Resources

Four switches with the sounds of fire engine, train, ambulance and police car pre-recorded and an image of each placed on top

Toy fire engine, train, ambulance and police car

MAIN

• Place the two switches in front of each child and show them the fire engine and the train.

• Model pressing the fire engine switch and pointing to the fire engine. Play with the fire engine until the sound stops.

• Offer the child the two switches. As they press a switch, offer them the corresponding toy. Once the sound has finished, say 'My turn' and take the toy back and offer the switches again.

• If the child is confident with this, remove the train and add the police car and ambulance to the selection.

• Repeat.

PLENARY

Press each switch one more time; as the sound ends, say 'Finished' and put it in the box. Repeat until all switches and toys are back in the box.

CONSOLIDATION ACTIVITIES

When you have the garage or small world toys out, put matching sounds on the switches so that the children can get used to a range of environmental sounds.

5. The Shop

Learning Objective

Emerging

Pupils know familiar places and what they are for.

Additional Skills

Visual: matching pictures to objects.

Social communication: working in a small group.

Attention: increasing attention to 5–7 minutes.

Fine motor: spreading butter and jam.

Resources

Computer and interactive whiteboard

Presentation slide with a simple street containing three familiar shops, such as fast food shop, toyshop and bakers

Props for each of the shops (e.g. child's meal box, a toy in a packet and a loaf of bread)

Visuals for each of the props

Butter

Jam

Knife and plate

MAIN

• On the interactive whiteboard, show your presentation slide of a simple street with three shops clearly displayed.

• Show the box of props to the children. Ask a child to choose a prop and ask them which shop they would get it from.

• Put the wrong prop at a shop; see if the children notice.

• Repeat for each of the props.

PLENARY

Once the children have matched the props to the image, use the bread to make jam sandwiches with the group. Supply visual instructions if this is appropriate to encourage the children to do as much as they can for themselves.

CONSOLIDATION ACTIVITIES

Set up a role play for one of the shops, with as many real-life props as possible. Model the different roles to support the children.

6. Room Hunt

Learning Objective

Emerging

Pupils know familiar places and people and what they are there for.

Additional Skills

Kinaesthetic: moving freely around the school environment.

Visual: associating an object/photo/symbol with a physical space.

Communication: understanding a photo/object/symbol carries meaning.

Resources

Objects/photos/symbols (this will depend on the child's level of understanding) for different rooms and areas around the school

MAIN

- To set up this activity place an object/photo/symbol of the next room to explore in each room you are going to ask the children to go to; for example, if aiming for the hall for assembly as the final room, place an object/photo/symbol for the hall in the sensory room, a object/photo/symbol of the sensory room in the library and have a object/photo/symbol of the library to give to the children.

- Explain to each child that we have to go the hall for assembly but we don't know how to get there!

- Give the child the object/photo/symbol and explain that first the child has to go the library for reading. Support the child to hold the object/photo/symbol and to find the library as independently as possible. Once there, place object/photo/symbol next to the room. Go into the library and read a book together.

- Then say we have to find the next room! Support the child to find the next object/photo/symbol for the sensory room for swinging.

- Again support the child to hold the object/photo/symbol and to find the sensory room as independently as possible.

- Once there, say 'The sensory room for swinging!' and child and adult explore the sensory room.

- Again say we have to find the next room to go to! Support the child to find the next object/photo/symbol for the hall for assembly and support the child to walk to the hall as independently as possible.

6. Room Hunt *cont.*

PLENARY

Once seated in the hall for assembly review the rooms the children visited and the activities they did there by looking again at the object/photo/symbol for the different rooms.

CONSOLIDATION ACTIVITIES

As part of daily routine show children object/photo/symbol of room they are going to e.g. the hall for assembly, the library for reading, the kitchen for cooking and support them to find their way there as independently as possible.

Teaching note: this 'room hunt' is only a suggested route with suggested activities; there are many different routes and activities that can be explored using this lesson plan.

7. Move Me

Learning Objective

Emerging

Pupils consolidate a sense of place and direction.

Additional Skills

Visual: matching picture to objects.

Social communication: working in a small group.

Attention: increasing attention to 5–7 minutes.

Fine motor: controlling the beebot.

Resources

Images of four familiar places to the children (school, park, train station, swimming pool)

Beebots (ideally one for each child)

Small images of the four familiar places in a bag

MAIN

- Place the images of four familiar places on the floor (north, east, south, west), roughly where they would be in relation to each other. For example, if your school is to the north of your town or village, place this north on the floor.

- Set a beebot in the middle of the images.

- Gather the children around the images on the floor. Model taking the first turn, pull an image out of the bag, look carefully, find the matching one on the floor and model saying the name, for example, 'school'.

- Go to the beebot and talk through, in key words, the steps to get the beebot to the location. Programme the beebot to get it to the school.

- Ask the children 'Who wants a turn?' Let everyone have some turns. If you have more than one beebot, one per person would be ideal.

Teaching note: if you have not used beebots with the children before, prior to this lesson, give them a chance to explore how the simple controls work. Make this lesson easier by only using two images at a time, so the beebot needs only to go forwards or backwards.

PLENARY

Place a box on its side. Ask the children to race their beebots back into the box. Who can get theirs in first?

CONSOLIDATION ACTIVITIES

Offer the beebots as a free choice activity. You could include a large 100 square and a set of numbers and the children need to direct the beebot to the correct number.

8. Find Me Fetch Me Dress Me

Learning Objective

Emerging

Pupils consolidate
a sense of place
and direction.

Additional Skills

Social communication:
working with a partner.

Kinaesthetic: moving
around the school.

Fine motor: dressing
a teddy.

Resources

A teddy bear or doll that
can be dressed

A range of clothing items
for the teddy or doll
with matching photos/
symbols of the items

Objects/photos/symbols
that represent familiar
rooms and locations
around the school

MAIN

• To set up this activity place the items of teddy/doll clothing in different rooms and locations around the school; for example, teddy's trousers in the playground.

• Support the children to choose a classmate to work with.

• Show the children the teddy/doll and explain we need to help them find their clothes!

• Show the children a photo/symbol of the first item of clothing to be found and then give the children the object/photo/symbol of the room or location where the item can be found.

• The children find the room or location, fetch the item, return to the classroom and dress the teddy/doll in the item of clothing.

• Repeat this until all the items of clothing have been found and the teddy/doll is fully dressed!

PLENARY

Once the teddy/doll has been dressed, ask the children to match the photo/symbol of the clothing items to the rooms or location object/photo/symbols where they were found.

CONSOLIDATION ACTIVITIES

This lesson could be repeated as a race between partners to dress different teddies/dolls. Each time this lesson is repeated, add more/new rooms and locations to support the children to become familiar with the school environment.

9. In the Woods or in the Town?

Learning Objective

Emerging

Pupils show their awareness of significant differences between specific physical/natural and human made features of places.

Additional Skills

Visual: recognising clear differences between specific features of objects.

Social communication: working as part of a small group.

Auditory: listening and responding to simple instructions.

Resources

Interactive whiteboard (IWB)

A video clip of a woodland that highlights natural/physical features of a woodland e.g. trees, birds, grass, flowers, insects

A video clip of a town that highlights human made features e.g. houses, shops, cars, road

An A3 background image of a woodland

MAIN

• Support the children to sit around the IWB ready to learn.

• Show the video clip of the woodland and label the physical/natural features e.g. trees, birds, grass, flowers, insects. Show the children the corresponding object/photo/symbol for each feature.

• Show the video clip of the town and label the human made features e.g. houses, shops, cars, road.

• Show the children the corresponding object/photo/symbol for each feature.

• On the floor in front of the IWB or at the table place the A3 background pictures of the woodland and town.

• Support the children to sort the objects/photos/symbols of physical/natural and human made features onto either the woodland or town picture.

• (Some might crossover e.g. birds, trees; this is a good opportunity to emphasise which features are natural and what are human made.)

PLENARY

Place the large 'natural' and 'human made' symbols in front of the children and support them to re-sort the feature object/photo/symbols onto them according to whether they are natural or human made.

9. In the Woods or in the Town? *cont.*

An A3 background image of a town

Objects/photos/symbols that correspond to the natural/physical features of a woodland and the human made features of a town

A large 'natural' symbol

A large 'human made' symbol

CONSOLIDATION ACTIVITIES

Go on a class walk to either a local town or woodland and see if the children can label natural and human made features using a symbol.

10. Where I Truly Belong

Learning Objective

Emerging

Pupils show their awareness of significant differences between natural and human made features of places.

Additional Skills

Visual: matching picture to objects.

Social communication: working in a small group.

Attention: increasing attention to 5–7 minutes.

Resources

Large image of a park

Large image of a school

Items that you would find in a park (e.g. leaves, ducks, grass, flowers) and school (e.g. computer, pencils, books, scissors)

MAIN

• Place a large picture of the park on one side of the circle and a large picture of a school on the other side of the circle.

• Ask the children to join you. Show them the basket of all of the small world items that you have collected along with the natural items you have found.

• Take out a model computer, look at it and ask 'Where do I belong?' Place it in the school.

• Take out a duck and ask the same question. Place it in the park.

• Take out a writing book and place it in the park; ask the question. You want a child to correct you and place it in the school.

• Give each of the children the basket and ask them to choose an item, asking, 'Where does it belong?'

• Once everyone has had a turn, look around your classroom and see if there are any other items the children would like to add.

PLENARY

Once the activity has finished, ask the children to first pack away the school, and take a look at the box. Then, to pack away the park, count down '5, 4, 3, 2, 1' to finish the activity.

CONSOLIDATION ACTIVITIES

Carry out this same lesson to consolidate the skill with other settings, such as a street and a forest, or a supermarket and a garden.

11. Wish You Were Here!

Learning Objective

Emerging

Pupils can answer simple questions about places.

Additional Skills

Visual: matching picture to objects.

Social communication: working in a small group.

Attention: increasing attention to 5–7 minutes.

Fine motor: putting on clothes.

Tactile: exploring a range of materials.

Resources

Pictures of a beach, skiing, city, boat trip, safari

Clothes to go with each (swimsuit, scarf or woolly hat, baseball cap, stripy top, beige jacket)

Props to go with each (sand, ice, brick, water, dry mud)

Access to a display board and Blu Tack or pins

MAIN

- Have all the pictures and clothes in a large box. Invite the children to join you.

- Tell them they are going to think about different places; some they may know and others may be new.

- Pull out a picture of the beach from the box. Ask the children, 'Have you been here before?' Pass around the tray of sand so that everyone can feel it.

- Ask the children, 'What do we wear at the beach?' Give two choices, a scarf or a swimsuit.

- Place the picture on the display board with the clothes that match.

- Let a child choose a picture from the box. Repeat the activity for everyone in the group.

PLENARY

Once everyone has had a turn, look at the display that has been made. What is everyone's favourite place?

CONSOLIDATION ACTIVITIES

Put some travel brochures next to the display and set up a travel agent with props such as passports, suitcases and plane tickets.

12. Where Do I Work?

Learning Objective

Emerging

Pupils can answer simple questions about places and people.

Additional Skills

Social communication: taking a turn as part of small group.

Communication: responding to simple questions through gesture/symbol/sign/speech.

Fine motor: developing independent dressing skills through exploring dressing up.

Resources

Interactive whiteboard (IWB)

Child-appropriate video clips of e.g. police officer in the police station, firefighter in the fire station, post person in the post office

A4 laminated pictures of the police station, fire station, post office

MAIN

- Support the children to come over to the IWB and be ready to learn.

- Play the video clips of, for example, police officer in the police station, firefighter in the fire station, post person in the post office. Use language such as 'The police officer works in the police station.' 'The firefighter works in the fire station.'

- On the floor in front of the IWB or at the table place the A4 laminated pictures of the police station, fire station, post office.

- Show the children the feely bag (which contains the small world figures) and sing the song, to the tune of 'Jingle Bells', 'Feely bag, feely bag, what's inside the feely bag? Put your hand in, feel about, when you're ready pull someone out!'

- The child pulls out a small world figure and the adult asks e.g. 'Where does the police officer work?' The child then places the small world figure onto the correct A4 laminated picture.

- Repeat until all the small world figures have been found in the feely bag and placed in their correct workplace.

PLENARY

Once all the small world figures have been sorted, the children take it in turns to choose their preferred person who helps us and then explore the dressing up clothes and role play props for their chosen person. Ask questions such as, 'What noise does your car make?', 'How do you use the hose?', 'How do you post a letter?'

12. Where Do I Work? *cont.*

Small world figures
of a police officer,
firefighter, post person
(if small world figures
are unavailable
use laminated
pictures instead)

Feely bag

Dressing up clothes
and role play props for
police officer, firefighter,
post person

CONSOLIDATION ACTIVITIES

When exploring different Geography topics explore
them in a similar way e.g. have a coastal scene and a
river scene and sort objects and items that belong in
those places.

13. Autumn Leaf Walk

Learning Objective

Emerging

Pupils start to sort and classify objects in terms of simple features or properties.

Additional Skills

Kinaesthetic: walking and moving in a different environment such as the park or woods.

Tactile: exploring the shape and texture of different outdoor features e.g. leaves, soil.

Social communication: completing a task as part of a small group.

Resources

Access to a local park or woods (including appropriate risk assessments)

Bags for leaf collection

A4 laminated colour symbols

Whiteboard and pens

Large rainbow template (big enough for classroom display)

Smaller colour symbols

Glue

MAIN

- In autumn term, go on a local walk through a park or woodland. Prepare the children beforehand using a simple story or slide show explaining that we are going on a walk in the park/woods to collect leaves!

- Whilst on the walk encourage the children to find and collect as many leaves as possible, commenting on them as the children find them e.g. 'That's a big yellow leaf!', 'This brown leaf is crunchy.'

- Once everyone is back in the classroom, support the children to work in small groups to explore the leaves they found and to sort them into colour groups using the A4 laminated colour symbols.

- If possible, use the whiteboards and pens to then count e.g. how many green leaves the children found and keep a tally.

PLENARY

Once all the leaves have been sorted, support the children to use the large rainbow template to make an autumn leaf rainbow by gluing the leaves according to colour onto the template and then label each arc using a smaller colour symbol. This could then be used as part of a class display about seasons or weather.

CONSOLIDATION ACTIVITIES

This lesson could be repeated and the leaves sorted by different criteria such as size. The children could then make a bar chart as part of a maths lesson.

14. Leaf Snap

Learning Objective

Emerging

Pupils start to sort and classify objects in terms of simple features.

Additional Skills

Visual: searching and locating requested items.

Attention: increasing attention to 5–7 minutes.

Tactile: exploring a range of materials.

Resources

Risk assessment

Plastic bags

Access to local walk

Big and small visuals for each child

Sugar paper and glue

MAIN

- Prior to this lesson, ensure you gain permission and carry out a risk assessment as per your school/setting requirements.

- Give each child a plastic bag and all go out for a nature walk. The best season is autumn, as you will find the most fallen leaves. Encourage the children to collect a variety of leaves.

- When back in class, give each child a set of big and small visuals.

- Model classifying the leaves by picking up two and deciding which is big and which is small.

- Ask the children to do the same.

- Once they have some that they have chosen and sorted, give each child sugar paper and glue and ask them to stick them down.

- Once everyone has finished, tidy away the remaining leaves and the glue.

PLENARY

Sitting around a table, ask the children to show their work. What was the biggest leaf they found? Can they find two that are identical?

CONSOLIDATION ACTIVITIES

Put the leftover leaves into a builder's tray and add some other items such as numbers or letters so that the children can continue to explore and sort the leaves and carry out a maths or English focus.

15. Natural or Made?

Learning Objective

Developing

Pupils understand the differences between physical/natural and human made features of places.

Additional Skills

Tactile: feeling different textures of objects.

Attention: taking part in an adult-led activity for 3–8 minutes.

Visual: noticing the difference between natural and made objects.

Resources

Builder's tray

A range of natural artefacts and materials found at the seaside e.g. shells, fossils, pebbles, salted water in a jug, sand, seaweed

A range of human made artefacts and materials found at the seaside e.g. bucket and spade, lollipop sticks, swimming trunks, boats

1 box labelled 'natural'

1 box labelled 'made'

MAIN

- To set up for this lesson make a seaside scenario in the builder's tray using the natural and made artefacts and materials. Place the two boxes on either side of the builder's tray.

- Support the children to come to the builder's tray and initially explore the seaside scenario. As the children explore, adult comments e.g. 'The sand is natural; the boat is made.'

- After a short while explain that now we need to put all the natural objects in one box, and all the made objects in another.

- Adult supports the children to sort the seaside artefacts and materials into the two boxes.

PLENARY

Adult asks the children to take one object at a time from either the natural or made box to remake the seaside scenario.

CONSOLIDATION ACTIVITIES

If possible, visit the seaside. While there ask the children about different features e.g. 'Is the bucket natural or made?' 'Is the seaweed natural or made?' Use symbols to support the children to answer.

16. Who Made It?

Learning Objective

Developing

Pupils understand the differences between the natural and made features of a place.

Additional Skills

Visual: noticing detail in a picture.

Communication: talking about a choice that has been made.

Attention: increasing attention to 7–10 minutes.

Fine motor: using a pen.

Resources

Access to a computer and the Internet

Large white paper

Natural and made visuals

Images of natural items (things that grow)

Images of made items

Picture of a park containing made and natural items for each child

Blue and green pens

MAIN

- Find a video on the Internet of things that grow. This could be a person, a tree, a plant. After the video, talk to the children about things that are natural, and how they grow.

- Put the key word 'natural' at the top of a piece of paper. Show the children a selection of images and ask them if they are natural or something different.

- Once you have a page of natural items, talk about things that are made. Show a brief video clip of a manufacturing process.

- Repeat the image selection activity for items that are made.

- Give each child a picture of a park that contains made items (slide, swings, bench, popcorn stand) and natural items (grass, ducks, river, flowers). Ask the children to draw a green circle around the natural items and a blue circle around the made items.

PLENARY

All come together as a group and look at each other's work. Did everyone choose the same or are there some things that are hard to decide?

CONSOLIDATION ACTIVITIES

Do an environmental walk around the school. Provide each child with a clipboard and sheet split in two columns – natural and made. How many items can the children find around the school?

17. I Went to the Shop and I Bought…

Learning Objective

Developing

Pupils use pictures or symbols to show familiar places and what they are for.

Additional Skills

Visual: noticing detail in a picture.

Communication: talking about a choice that has been made.

Attention: increasing attention to 7–10 minutes.

Resources

Pictures of familiar high street shops

Small images of what you can buy in the shop (one for each child for each shop)

Blu Tack

Shopping list for each child

Basket or bag for each child

MAIN

- Place the pictures of familiar high street shops around the room. On each of the pictures, with Blu Tack, stick on the item of what you can buy there (one for each child).

- Ask the children to gather around. Tell them that they need to 'go shopping'. Give each child a shopping list and a basket (or bag).

- With minimal adult support, encourage the children to explore the room and the different shops.

- Who can complete their shopping list first?

- Once everyone has their shopping, as a group each child shows what they 'bought'.

PLENARY

Read out the name of an item, and the children all walk over to the shop from which the item would be bought. Each child should get a turn at leading the game.

CONSOLIDATION ACTIVITIES

Play this game a few times as a group, and then offer it as a free choice activity. The children can set it up themselves and give out the shopping lists.

18. Where Shall I Sit?

Learning Objective

Developing

Pupils use pictures or symbols to make simple plans and maps of familiar places.

Additional Skills

Social communication: interacting and sitting with other children.

Communication: communicating their ideas to others.

Resources

A3 template of lunch table

Small photos of classmates the child will sit with at lunchtime

Glue

MAIN

- Explain to the children that we need to think about where everyone sits at lunchtime and we need the children's help to make a plan.

- Show the children the lunch table template and model making a seating plan by placing the small photos of their classmates around the table.

- Then support each child to make a seating plan of their own.

- Once the child is happy with their seating plan, support them to use the glue to stick the photos onto the plan so it can be used at lunchtime.

PLENARY

At lunchtime, support each child to use their seating plan to help all the children find their places at the table following the seating plan the child has made.

CONSOLIDATION ACTIVITIES

Children could make seating plans for different times of their day e.g. group work, circle time, assembly. This could also be extended to play activities such as making a seating plan for a teddy bear tea party, or a seating plan for a pretend aeroplane trip!

19. Today, I Am...

Learning Objective

Developing

Pupils show what they think about different people and answer simple questions.

Additional Skills

Communication: asking and answering questions.

Attention: increasing attention to 7–10 minutes.

Fine motor: dressing and undressing skills.

Resources

A selection of 'people who help me' dressing up clothes and props

Question prompt cards (if needed)

MAIN

- Sitting as a group, place all of the dressing up items in the centre.

- Ask the children to choose the outfit or prop that they want to wear and put it on.

- Work around the group while the children are doing this, asking questions such as 'Who are you?', 'Who do you help?', 'Where do you work?'

- Once everyone is dressed up, ask each child in turn to tell the group what they chose to wear and what their job or role is.

- Encourage the children to ask a question; they can use question prompt sheets if helpful.

- Take 2–3 turns at choosing different items and speaking and listening.

PLENARY

After the last turn, ask all the children to take off their dressing up clothes and put them back in the box.

CONSOLIDATION ACTIVITIES

Play a clues game with the children. Hide a prop in a box and give the children clues such as, 'I work in a hospital', 'I help people when they are sick', 'I work with doctors'. Hopefully they guess a nurse! Other examples could include placing a firefighter's hat in the box and saying 'I use water in my job', 'I help people when there is a fire', 'I go down a pole when I hear the alarm'.

20. Over Here or There?

Learning Objective

Developing

Pupils show what they think about different environments and answer simple questions about places.

Additional Skills

Tactile: experiencing different sensory environments.

Communication: using symbols/speech or sign to make a comment to another person.

Social communication: taking part in an experience as part of a small group.

Resources

Resources to make an earthquake area e.g. chairs, mats

Resources to make a river environment e.g. blue material, water sprays

Laminated 'Like' and 'Don't like' symbols

Laminated symbols to support children's commenting

MAIN

- Set up two different 'environment' areas in the classroom e.g. an earthquake area where children sit on chairs that the adults shake, making a lot of noise; a river area with blue material and water sprays that the adults use to spray on the children as if they were in a river.

- Support the children to go to each area and experience the environment.

- Support the children to comment, using laminated cards if necessary e.g. like/don't like the water, and to answer simple questions such as, 'Is this area wet or dry?'

PLENARY

Once the children have experienced both areas encourage them to choose an environment to go back to and explore again. Support the children to comment on their choice e.g. 'I like the earthquake.'

CONSOLIDATION ACTIVITIES

Repeat this lesson but set up different 'environments' e.g. use soft play equipment to make a mountain and use fans to represent the windy top of the mountain, use a heater and sand to make desert environment. Once the children have experienced several different environments set up three or four of them again in the classroom and support the children to make a choice for their favourite/least favourite and to answer simple questions about the different environments.

21. Build-a-Town

Learning Objective

Developing

Pupils communicate their preferences about the physical/natural and human/made features of places.

Additional Skills

Social communication: taking turns with a peer.

Communication: expressing and communicating a preference.

Attention: maintaining focus and attention on an adult-led activity for 10 minutes.

Resources

Builder's tray

Small world representations of natural and human/made features e.g. trees, grass, rocks, plants, swings, library building, houses, cars.

1 box labelled 'natural'

1 box labelled 'made'

Laminated 'Like' and 'Don't like' symbols

MAIN

- To set up this activity sort the small world representations of natural and human made features into the appropriate 'natural' and 'made' boxes and place next to the builder's tray.

- Support each child and a partner to come over to the builder's tray.

- Explain that today we are going to build our own town by choosing the features we 'like' (shows the symbol) and 'don't like' (shows the symbol).

- Model choosing a feature and adding to the builder's tray to start building the town e.g. say 'I like houses' and then find the small world representation of the house and place it in the builder's tray to start to build the town.

- Support the children to take it in turns to choose a feature to add to the town and to express their preference using symbols/speech/sign.

PLENARY

Once the town has been built encourage the children to play with small world figures in the town. When it is time for the activity to finish support the children to first sort the features onto the 'Like' and 'Don't like' symbols and then into the appropriate box, either the 'natural' box or 'made' box.

CONSOLIDATION ACTIVITIES

Repeat this lesson and once the town has been built support the children to make a simple map of their town by drawing or using symbols. Support the children to label the features 'natural' or 'made' and indicate their preference using speech/signs or symbols.

22. My Choice

Learning Objective

Developing

Pupils communicate their preferences about the natural and human made features of places.

Additional Skills

Visual: noticing detail in a picture.

Communication: using a complete sentence.

Attention: increasing attention to 7–10 minutes.

Resources

Images of places around the world (London landmarks, beach, parks, forest train stations, etc.)

Whiteboard and pen

Slips of paper and pen for adult

Access to display board

MAIN

- Have the photos of the places to hand and ask the children to join you.

- On the board write 'I like the ……………'

- Model looking through the pictures and choosing one, showing the rest of the group and completing the sentence. This can be done with visuals if the child does not yet have verbal language.

- Hand a set of photos to each child; ask them to choose their favourite place.

- Once everyone has chosen, go around the group so everyone can say their sentence.

- Get an adult to scribe each of the children's sentences.

- To make this lesson a little harder extend the sentence e.g. 'I like the park *because* the grass feels nice to walk on.'

- Ask the children if they can add a '*because*' to their sentence. Adult should scribe these sentences also.

PLENARY

All go to a board and give the children Blu Tack so that they can place their picture and their sentence on the display.

CONSOLIDATION ACTIVITIES

During an ICT lesson, encourage the children to look for more pictures of the place that they chose to add to the display.

Teaching note: if visual support is needed, make symbol sentences that the children can complete e.g. 'I like ………. because ……..' and make a range of symbols that the children can choose from to complete the sentence.

23. Playground Planning

Learning Objective

Developing

Pupils can represent and record key features of a place using models or symbols.

Additional Skills

Fine motor: using controlled movements to use a camera or tablet to take a photo.

Visual: noticing the detail of areas of the playground.

Communication: indicating to another person where to place an item such as a photo.

Resources

Tablet or camera

Large playground template

Small world toy representations of playground equipment (if possible) e.g. slide, swing

Symbols of playground equipment

MAIN

- Explain to a small group of children that today we are going to make a map of the playground.

- Support the children to go to the playground, look around at where the equipment is placed and to take photos of the playground as they explore.

- Back in classroom, lay out the large playground template.

- Support the children to work together to refer to their photos to use the small world representation and/or symbols of playground equipment to mark key playground features on the template.

- All together, go back to the playground with the completed map and support the children to comment on the accuracy of their map.

- Film the children going outside and using map to find different features of playground.

PLENARY

Back in classroom look at video of children using map and comment on how accurate their map was. Do they think their map is better than what is in the playground?

CONSOLIDATION ACTIVITIES

Repeat this method for other areas of the school such as the classroom, lunch hall, etc.

24. Recycle Me Do

Learning Objective

Developing

Pupils are aware of their role in caring for their own environment.

Additional Skills

Attention: recalling events from previous lesson to complete a task.

Tactile: handling different textured items.

Visual: understanding different symbols have different meanings.

Resources

Interactive whiteboard (IWB) or tablet

Video clips about how rubbish affects the environment

A range of recyclable rubbish materials

Large laminated symbols for common recyclable materials e.g. paper, plastic

A box for each recyclable material to be explored

MAIN

- Support a small group of children to sit with a view of the IWB or tablet to view some short video clips about how rubbish affects the environment; for example, plastic in the oceans, rubbish in woodlands.

- At the table, support the children to explore different materials that make up recyclable rubbish e.g. paper, plastic, tin.

- Model identifying a recyclable material e.g. paper, and placing it onto the correct laminated symbol.

- The children then sort through the rubbish, identifying the material and sorting it onto the correct symbol.

- Once this is done, support the children to place the rubbish into the correctly labelled box for that material.

- In the next Geography lesson the children walk into the classroom to find their table covered in 'rubbish'!

- Explain that it all needs recycling and support them to sort the rubbish on their tables into the respective recycling boxes.

PLENARY

Once all the rubbish has been sorted, as a group look through the boxes and check that there are no mistakes.

CONSOLIDATION ACTIVITIES

Support a small group of children to be in charge of recycling for their year group by going to collect rubbish from other classrooms and sorting it into the correct recycling boxes.

25. All Help Together

Learning Objective

Developing

Pupils are aware of their role in caring for their own environment.

Additional Skills

Social communication: understanding that we take turns.

Attention: increasing attention to 7–10 minutes.

Resources

Large white paper

Marker pens

MAIN

- Carry out an environmental walk of the school. Point out to the children the things that need looking after, such as plants and flowers, animals, picking up litter, collecting lost property and tidying the book corner.

- Back in class, ask the children to name all the things that we can do to look after the school environment. Write these on a big sheet of paper.

- Tell the children that each one of them is going to have a responsibility for the week to carry out one of these tasks, each child to select the task they want. If more than one child wants the task, negotiate and offer them the chance next week.

- Working individually, ask each child what they need in order to carry out the task they have been allocated.

- Allocate time each day so that the children can carry out their tasks.

- At the end of the week, talk about what they have done and if they feel that they helped make the school a better place.

PLENARY

Pin the responsibility board up in the class so that the children can see this; add a tick column so that everyone can see how often the task has been done.

CONSOLIDATION ACTIVITIES

Encourage the children to think of more tasks that could be added, such as helping with the recycling, or tucking the chairs in to keep everyone safe.

26. Follow the Arrows

Learning Objective

Developing

Pupils begin to use symbols to represent direction.

Additional Skills

Social communication: working collaboratively.

Attention: increasing attention to 7–10 minutes.

Resources

Laminated direction arrows (enough for each group to have 5–6)

MAIN

- Put the children in pairs; this could be with an adult or a peer.

- Tell the children that today is all about directions, but that we cannot use our voices.

- Model the first turn. Point to a part of the room they would like the other person to get to (such as the computer). Place arrows on the floor that the other person can follow to get to the computer. Pick up the arrows. Then choose one more location and repeat.

- Give each group a set of arrows and ask them to direct their partner around the room.

PLENARY

The last turn is going to be using voice, using language such as 'forwards', 'left', 'right' and 'backwards'. If this is too challenging, just use forwards and backwards as direction terms.

CONSOLIDATION ACTIVITIES

Set up an obstacle course outside and, working in pairs, give each group the set of arrows so that they can direct the order that they want their partner to complete the course.

27. Roll-a-Feature

Learning Objective

Securing

Pupils can recognise the physical/natural and human made features of places.

Additional Skills

Gross motor: respond to a visual prompt to make a large movement.

Communication: understanding that a symbol carries meaning.

Visual: recognising if a symbol represents something made or natural.

Resources

Large pocket dice with symbols of made and natural features of e.g. a town, such as cars, roads, trees, flowers

Large laminated 'natural' and 'made' symbols

MAIN

- Support a small group of children to come and sit in a semicircle ready to learn.

- Place the large laminated 'natural' and 'made' symbols on either side of the semicircle.

- Model rolling the dice, reading out the symbol it lands on, for example, car and then running to the 'made' symbol.

- Support the children to take a turn rolling the dice and identifying if the feature is made or natural.

PLENARY

Once all the children have had one or two turns each, remove the feature symbols dice, place the 'natural' and 'made' symbols at either end of the semicircle, and ask the children to push back their chairs (if they were sat on them). Then show the group a feature symbol e.g. a tree, and as a group the children run to either the 'made' or 'natural' laminated symbols.

CONSOLIDATION ACTIVITIES

When out in the community, ask the child simple questions about features in the environment e.g. 'Is the grass natural or made?'

28. Mark It Down

Learning Objective

Securing

Pupils recognise the natural and made features of places.

Additional Skills

Social communication: understanding that we take turns.

Attention: increasing attention to 10–15 minutes.

Fine motor: making tally marks.

Resources

Cards that have 'natural' and 'made' for each child

Video clip of a journey or tour through a town (or a book if this cannot be sourced)

Clipboard and pens

Tally sheet with the headings 'natural' and 'made'

MAIN

- Give each child two cards, one that says 'natural' and one that says 'made'. Explain what these terms mean and provide some examples.

- If using a video, play the video and ask the children to raise the appropriate card when they see either a made or natural item.

- Once the video is over, pair the children up. Ask one to hold the cards, and the other to keep a tally. Whenever the first child holds up a card, the second gives it a tally mark.

- At the end of the video, swap over.

PLENARY

Once each child has taken a turn, talk about what you saw, and how many natural and made items were present.

CONSOLIDATION ACTIVITIES

Print the words 'natural' and 'made' onto stickers. Ask the children to go around the room and place the stickers on the items that they can find.

29. Who Am I?

Learning Objective

Securing

Pupils can use resources given to them and their own observations to respond to simple questions about people.

Additional Skills

Social communication: taking part in a role play as part of a group.

Visual: identifying similarities between actions, visual cues and a familiar role.

Communication: using symbol, speech or sign to communicate an answer to a familiar phrase or question.

Resources

Laminated symbols of people who help us e.g. firefighter, police officer, doctor, nurse (a set per child)

Dressing up and role play items related to people who help us

MAIN

- Support children to come as part of a small group to sit in a semicircle ready to learn.

- Give each child a set of the laminated symbols of people who help us.

- Quickly dress up as a person who helps us and acts out part of their role e.g. puts on a fire helmet and mimes putting out a fire.

- Ask 'Who am I?' The first child to use a symbol/speech/sign to answer wins!

- The winner is then the next person to dress up as a person who helps us and act out part of their role for the group. Adult may need to support the child to ask the question 'Who am I?'

- Repeat this until all the children have had a turn acting out a person who helps us.

PLENARY

Once all the children have had a turn ask each child to choose a person who helps us and support them to dress up and engage in role play with each other acting as their chosen person. Adult can ask simple questions such as, 'Who are you?', 'What job do you do?'

CONSOLIDATION ACTIVITIES

When out in the community, support the children to spot people who help us and ask simple questions e.g. if you see a postman ask the children questions such as 'What job does he do?', 'Where does he work?'

30. It's a Wide Wide World

Learning Objective

Securing

Pupils recognise simple symbols or representations on simple maps and plans.

Additional Skills

Visual: recognising and naming familiar landmarks.

Fine motor: using one or two fingers to control a tablet screen.

Communication: commenting using symbols/speech/sign to another person.

Resources

Access to the Internet

Interactive whiteboard (IWB)

Tablet per child/per pair

A4 plain paper

Range of coloured crayons

MAIN

- Support the children to sit with a view of the IWB ready to learn.

- Use a map program on the Internet to show the children the earth; do they know what our planet is called?

- In the search bar type the name of the country the children live in e.g. the United Kingdom, and ask the children to comment.

- Then search for e.g. the county, the town or city and eventually the school, each time asking the children to comment on landmarks, buildings or on representations. For instance, they may comment on large areas of green or blue.

- Give each child or pair a tablet and ask them to type the name of the school/the name of the road they live on, etc. into an Internet-based map program.

- Support the children to comment on what they can see on the map.

PLENARY

Once the children have explored local areas using the tablet, ask each child to choose a favourite e.g. the local park, and make a representation of this map using the paper and coloured crayons. The children could then share their maps with the group, describing the simple representations they have used on their maps.

CONSOLIDATION ACTIVITIES

When learning about new topics and/or environments in Geography, such as volcanoes, support children to use the tablets and the Internet-based map program to explore maps of these areas. Support children to understand and learn new simple symbols and representations on maps of different areas and environments.

31. Take Me There

Learning Objective

Securing

Pupils recognise simple symbols or representations on maps and plans.

Additional Skills

Social communication: sharing space with others.

Attention: increasing attention to 10–15 minutes.

Visual: directing the beebot.

Resources

Large paper

Pictures of landmarks

Symbols

Beebot for each child

List of symbols for each child

MAIN

- Prior to the lesson, cover the floor with paper; draw a grid on it with letters across the top and numbers down the side. Place pictures of landmarks on the paper, and put a symbol next to each that would correspond to a map symbol, such as a cross for a church or an ambulance for a hospital.

- When the children are in class, give each of them a beebot and a list of symbols. Each child needs to direct their beebot to the correct symbol, and then write the name of the building or landmark that they found.

Teaching note: if children have not used beebots before, then you will need to teach them prior to this session.

PLENARY

Give a building name to each of the children and ask them to direct their beebot to it. Pick up the image and the beebot and return it to the box.

CONSOLIDATION ACTIVITIES

Set this up again and ask the children to provide the symbols or landmarks to other children.

32. Land, Air and Sea

Learning Objective

Securing

Pupils use simple geographical language to communicate their ideas about various locations.

Additional Skills

Social communication: sharing learning with another person.

Attention: increasing attention to 10–15 minutes.

Visual: matching the correct object.

Tactile: exploring a range of real and made materials.

Resources

Large box for the resources

Small world resources (land: soil, grass, land animals, buildings, trees, etc.) (air: cotton wool clouds, birds, stars, airplane, kite, moon, etc.) (sea: water, seaweed, fish, shells, etc.)

Pictures of land, air and sea

Three builder's trays

MAIN

• Place a large box with the resources for the small world play in front of the children. Tell them that one of the younger classes asked for their help in making some play activities on land, sea and air.

• Ask the children if they know what these terms mean.

• Show the children a picture that corresponds to each of the headings.

• Place each picture in a builder's tray and tell the children they need to think carefully about what items they might find on land, in the sea and in the air.

• Set out the box of resources and give the children time to create small world play trays.

PLENARY

Once all the resources are placed, check the items to make sure they match. If there are any misplaced items, ask the children to consider this. Allow the children time to play with the small world trays.

CONSOLIDATION ACTIVITIES

Invite some younger children to come and play so that the group can explain to them about land, air and sea environments.

33. This Is Pretty

Learning Objective

Securing

Pupils express their views on features of the environment they find attractive or unattractive.

Additional Skills

Communication: voicing an opinion.

Attention: increasing attention to 10–15 minutes.

Visual: noticing features.

Resources

Attractive and unattractive cards

Large images of features of the environment

Page of images from the environment

Plain paper

Glue

Scissors

MAIN

- Explain to the children what the terms 'attractive' and 'unattractive' mean, and that we don't all have to agree.

- Give each child two cards, one attractive and the other not attractive.

- Show the children the first image; ask them to make their choice and explain their choice.

- Repeat with three more images.

- Take a walk around the school and consider different features, such as the recycling and rubbish storage, the garden, the coat rack, the playground, and ask children to express their views about each feature.

PLENARY

Back in class, present the children with a page of images and a piece of paper with the headings 'attractive' and 'unattractive'. Give the children time to cut out the images and make a choice about how they want to categorise them. Use the glue to stick the images in the columns they have chosen to categorise them in.

CONSOLIDATION ACTIVITIES

Ask the children if there is any way to make some of the unattractive features of the school environment more attractive.

HISTORY

34. Here I Am!

Learning Objective

Emerging

Pupils can recognise themselves and other people in pictures of the recent past.

Additional Skills

Visual: recognising themselves and others in photographs.

Social communication: responding to another person.

Auditory: listening and responding to a familiar song.

Resources

Laminated photos of the child and other classmates from the very recent past

Choosing board

MAIN

- To set up the activity place the children's laminated photos on the choosing board and place chairs in a semicircle.

- Support the children to come and sit in the semicircle ready to learn.

- Sing to the tune of 'Tommy Thumb' using child's name, for example, William: 'William, William, where are you?'

- Give the child time to indicate where they are through gesture or vocalisation.

- Show the child the choosing board and support them to find their photo and sing, 'There you are! There you are! How do you do?' and shake the child's hand.

- Support the child to choose a photo of a friend and find that friend in the semicircle while the song is sung again.

- Repeat this until all the children in the circle have been sung to.

PLENARY

Ask the children to collect the photos from each child in the circle and place the photos back on the board for another turn.

CONSOLIDATION ACTIVITIES

Across the day support the children to recognise themselves in photos in their environment e.g. by finding their photo by their peg to hang up their coat/bag. Once the children are familiar with their own photo support them to identify a familiar friend by asking them to collect their friend's coat from their peg, etc.

35. It's Me!

Learning Objective

Emerging

Pupils recognise themselves and other people in pictures of the recent past.

Additional Skills

Visual: noticing themselves in a picture.

Attention: focusing on an activity for 5–7 minutes (or more).

Resources

Mirror for each child

Photos of individuals and groups of the children and adults

Photo album

MAIN

- This lesson needs to be carried out following a significant event, such as a trip or an activity in school. Take lots of pictures during the event ready for the lesson.

- Line up tables so that each child has a space to sit. Place mirrors at each place and allow the child time to explore their face.

- Remove the mirrors and ask them to look at each other.

- Give each child a photo of themselves; allow them time to look at this.

- While the child is looking at their photo, place a selection of photos on a separate table. Ask the children to come over and see who they can find.

PLENARY

Ask each child to find a photo of themselves to put in the album. Once everyone has taken a turn, count down and finish the lesson.

CONSOLIDATION ACTIVITIES

Place photos of the children and adults in a talking photo album. Record the people's names so that as the children explore, they can hear the name of the person they are looking at.

36. Summer or Winter?

Learning Objective

Emerging

Pupils can link the passage of time with a variety of indicators.

Additional Skills

Gross motor: using a big motion to roll a large pocket dice.

Tactile: experiencing different sensory media.

Social communication: taking a turn in a small group.

Resources

Large pocket dice with 'summer' and 'winter' symbols

Sunglasses

Small tray of sand

Heated hand warmer (if possible)

Woolly hat

Gloves

Shaving foam

Frozen ice pack (if possible)

Pictures of the child in summer clothes/situation and winter clothes/situation

MAIN

• Support a small group of children to sit in a semicircle ready to learn.

• Support the child to roll the pocket dice. Identify and verbally label which season the dice lands on.

• If the dice lands on 'summer' give the child sunglasses to wear and sand to feel (and the heated hand warmer if available).

• Sing, to the tune of 'Farmer's in the Den', 'In the summer it's hot! In the summer it's hot! See how the sun shines in the summer, it is hot!'

• If available, show the child a photo of them dressed in summer clothes in summertime.

• If the dice lands on winter give the child the woolly hat and gloves to wear and clap the shaving foam to make snow (explore the frozen ice pack if available).

• Sing, to the tune of 'Farmer's in the Den', 'In the winter it's cold, brrrr brrrr! In the winter it's cold, brrrr brrrr! See how the snow falls in the winter, it is cold!' If available, show the child a picture of themselves dressed in winter clothes.

• Support every child in the group to take a turn.

PLENARY

When all the children have had a turn, take out a summer symbol and winter symbol from the pocket dice and place them on the floor in front of the children. Give each child their winter and summer picture and support them to sort them onto the correct symbol.

CONSOLIDATION ACTIVITIES

Once the children are familiar with summer and winter introduce autumn and spring to the game.

37. Days of the Week

Learning Objective

Emerging

Pupils link the passage of time with a variety of indicators.

Additional Skills

Visual: matching a visual to an event.

Attention: focusing on an activity for 5–7 minutes (or more).

Social communication: using key words.

Resources

Access to a board (display board or whiteboard)

Laminated days of the week visuals

Laminated activity cards (swimming, cooking, trip, assembly, etc.)

Blu Tack if the visuals have not been Velcroed

MAIN

- On a Monday morning, work with the children to establish the plan for the week.

- Model placing the days of the week (including the weekend) on the board. (Eventually the child can do this.)

- Show the children visuals of familiar, regular activities that happen in the week, such as assembly, swimming, music, cooking, etc. Ask everyone, what do we do on Monday? Then place the matching visual.

- If there is anything different happening that week, such as a trip, or a visit from the dentist, include this too.

- On Saturday and Sunday, have pictures of 'no school' and place these with the symbol.

- Once this activity has been carried out a few times, keep the symbols for the week and on a Monday ask the children to think about the week before, prior to creating the timetable for this week coming.

PLENARY

Ask the children which activity they are looking forward to taking part in that week.

CONSOLIDATION ACTIVITIES

Over time, add the dates and months to the board so that the children can see that we use numbers to count how many days there are.

38. Feely Bag Routine

Learning Objective

Emerging

Pupils can use single words, signs or symbols to confirm the function of everyday items from the past.

Additional Skills

Visual: recognising an item from daily routine.

Attention: taking part in an adult-led activity for 5–7 minutes.

Social communication: engaging in activity with a familiar adult or peer.

Resources

Variety of items from the child's everyday routine e.g. cup, plate, small school bus, small representation of a bed

Feely bag

Photos of child using the object (use generic photo of object being used if photo unavailable)

MAIN

- Adult supports the child to sit opposite them.
- Sing the feely bag song (to the tune of 'Jingle Bells'): 'Feely bag, feely bag, what's inside the feely bag? Put your hand in, feel about, when you're ready pull something out!'
- Support the child to put their hand in the feely bag and pull out an item.
- Adult verbally labels the item and shows the child the picture of them using it.
- Both adult and child then mime using the everyday item.
- Repeat this until all of the items have been pulled from the feely bag.

PLENARY

Once all the objects have been taken out of the feely bag and placed on the table support the children to place them in order of their daily routine along with the appropriate photo. You could explain that the children did this yesterday, today and will do it again tomorrow.

CONSOLIDATION ACTIVITIES

Make a photo book using the photos from the activity in daily routine order and look at it with the children at different times of the day. Have the book available in the book corner or around the classroom for the children to explore independently.

39. That's Old

Learning Objective

Emerging

Pupils use single words, signs or symbols to confirm the function of everyday items from the past.

Additional Skills

Visual: matching a visual to an object.

Attention: focusing on activity for 5–7 minutes (or more).

Social communication: using key words.

Resources

Familiar old items (mobile phones, packaging, books, toys, etc.)

Symbols for each of the items

MAIN

- Prior to the lesson, gather as many 'old' familiar items as you can.

- Tell the children that it is a history lesson, and that in history you learn about the past.

- Show the group the first item; does anyone know what this is? Allow everyone to touch it and encourage them to role play using it.

- Place this on a table and put down the symbol that matches it.

- Continue with the other items.

- Once all items are on the table, ask a child to find one of them; see if they can do this.

- Repeat for the group.

- For the next turn, ask them to choose one and tell you the name (or sign or use the symbol).

PLENARY

Pack the items away and count down for the lesson to finish.

CONSOLIDATION ACTIVITIES

Place the old items on an interactive display with new items that match. Place the symbols in a pot and ask the children to label the display.

40. Assembly Remembering

Learning Objective

Emerging

Pupils know they took part in past events and they listen and respond to stories about their own past.

Additional Skills

Social communication: taking part in an activity with a small group.

Communication: responding to watching themselves on video using sign/symbol/speech.

Attention: taking part in a group activity for 5–7 minutes (or more).

Resources

Tablet/camera

Topic-related role play items and dressing up clothes

MAIN

• Support the children to choose two or three classmates to form a small group.

• In the group, supported by the adult, develop a short play based on the class history topic to perform in the class assembly.

• Support the children to learn their part in the play.

• Perform the play as part of a class assembly for the whole school or key stage and ensure that an adult is available to film the children taking part in their play.

PLENARY

Watch back the video of the assembly with the children and support them to comment on what they are seeing; ask the children simple questions such as, 'What did you say?', 'Was assembly yesterday or today?', 'Who can you see?' Make it clear that the assembly happened in the past.

CONSOLIDATION ACTIVITIES

Repeat this lesson for new history topics to support the children to learn and recount actions or speech as part of a short play and then to watch the video back to understand that the play happened in the past. Also, if the children takes part or has taken part in other school events that have been filmed, such as Christmas plays, watch these with the children pointing out differences in them between then and now.

41. This One Time

Learning Objective

Emerging

Pupils listen and respond to familiar stories about their own past.

Additional Skills

Visual: noticing themselves in a picture.

Attention: focusing on an activity for 5–7 minutes (or more).

Social communication: sharing an experience with an adult and peer.

Resources

Letter to family to request story and pictures

Visuals to support answering questions (if needed)

MAIN

• Prior to this lesson, send a note home to each family asking for them to send in details of a memorable family story with pictures.

• Working one to one or in pairs, show the children the pictures and tell them the story. Leave pauses to see if they can insert names or locations or point to people in the pictures.

• If working in pairs, then both children can enjoy listening to the other's story.

• Ask questions such as 'What did you do?', 'How did you feel?' and have visuals to support the answering of the question.

PLENARY

Thank the children for sharing the story and count down from 5 to 0 to indicate the activity has finished.

CONSOLIDATION ACTIVITIES

Create a class short story book from the stories and pictures that the families have sent in. During a reading session, the children can choose this as one of the books they read and share.

42. Adult or Baby?

Learning Objective

Emerging

Pupils can begin to communicate about activities and events in the recent past in response to personal items from their own early childhood.

Additional Skills

Visual: recognising the difference between a baby item and an adult item.

Kinaesthetic: moving around the carpet area to sort the items.

Communication: making a choice between items.

Resources

Baby doll

Willing adult!

Selection of clearly adult and baby items e.g. baby clothes, adult clothes, cup, baby bottle

MAIN

- On the carpet or in a quiet space, present the children with the different items and verbally label them.

- Show the children the baby; model choosing an appropriate item and giving it to the baby.

- Then model choosing an appropriate item and give it to yourself (or another adult if available).

- Then encourage the children to explore the different objects and decide whether they are for the baby or the adult.

- Make a big show of not being a baby if you are given the wrong item.

PLENARY

Once the children have sorted all the items, support them to make a choice between the adult and baby symbols. They can then role play with their chosen person by dressing up the baby, giving the adult a drink in the cup, etc.

CONSOLIDATION ACTIVITIES

If possible, obtain photos of the children as a baby using some of the items that they have explored e.g. the children drinking from a bottle, wearing small clothes, etc. Share the photos with the children and comment on them.

43. How Rome Was Built

Learning Objective

Emerging

Pupils begin to communicate about activities and events in the past.

Additional Skills

Visual: recognising old and new items.

Attention: focusing on an activity for 5–7 minutes (or more).

Social communication: noticing a feature of an item.

Resources

Story of Romulus and Remus (from the Internet)

Basket for props

Selection of old props (wooden cup, hessian fabric, rope belt, gold coins, etc.)

Selection of modern props (plastic cup, t-shirt, £5 note, hairbrush, etc.)

Visuals for 'old' and 'new'

MAIN

- Read the children a simple version of the story of Romulus and Remus and how Rome was created; you can find this on the Internet.

- After reading the story, place a basket of props in front of the children.

- Ask them to find something that Romulus and Remus might have used (something old).

- Then ask the children to find something that they use every day.

- Place the visuals for 'old' and 'new' on the table and ask the children to sort the items.

PLENARY

Have a look at the items; would the children like to use any of the old items?

CONSOLIDATION ACTIVITIES

Create a sensory story prop bag to go with the story of Romulus and Remus; this can include water spray bottles, the sound of a baby crying, wool, etc.

44. How We Travelled

Learning Objective

Emerging

With some prompting or support pupils can answer simple questions about historical artefacts.

Additional Skills

Attention: taking part in a small group activity for 5–7 minutes (or more).

Gross and fine motor: using scissor and building skills to junk model a vehicle.

Communication: communicating a choice to a familiar adult or classmate.

Resources

Interactive whiteboard (IWB)

Photos and/or video clips of modern forms of transport e.g. planes, cars, modern bike, trains

Photos and/or video clips of older forms of transport e.g. blimp, horse and cart, penny-farthing

Large piece of material

Laminated 'past' and 'now' symbols

Junk modelling materials (boxes, tape, scissors, etc.)

MAIN

- Support a small group of children to sit in a semicircle facing the IWB.

- Look at the photos/short video clips of the ways we travel now and explain that this is how we get to school/home/shops now.

- With another adult, waft the large piece of material over the children to indicate going back in time (you may want to use music or sound effects to enhance this effect).

- Look at photos/short video clips of ways used to travel and explain that this is how people got to school/the shops/their houses in the past.

- Support the children to work together to sort the photos of the transport vehicles onto the 'now' and 'past' symbols.

PLENARY

Support the children to work in pairs to choose a favourite way to travel from either the past or now. Use the junk modelling materials to make the chosen vehicle and use them for role play. Encourage the children to comment on each other's work e.g. if their chosen vehicle is from the past or now.

CONSOLIDATION ACTIVITIES

Repeat this lesson to introduce other topics and the concept of things being different in the past to now e.g. seaside holidays.

45. No Plastic Here

Learning Objective

Emerging

Pupils, with some support, answer simple questions about historical buildings.

Additional Skills

Visual: recognising old and new items.

Attention: focusing on an activity for 5–7 minutes (or more).

Social communication: answering a question.

Tactile: exploring materials.

Resources

Pictures from a trip to a historical building

Visual headings: 'plastic', 'wood', 'metal'

Piece of wood, metal and plastic (all child safe)

MAIN

- If your local area contains any buildings that are historical or significant, take the children on a trip (ensure risk assessment and school policy followed) to provide the children with a first-hand experience. A church or place of worship is often old and accessible. Take photos of different features and of the children exploring.

- Back in class, show the children a picture of the building that they explored. (If this was not possible, show a picture of a building of your choice.)

- Ask them what it was called and what they remember about it.

- Present the children with three visual headings: 'plastic', 'wood' and 'metal'.

- Show the children the pictures of what they were exploring and ask them 'What is it made of?' and then match the appropriate label.

- Have samples of plastic, metal and wood that the children can hold and explore throughout; this is so that they can remember the textures and materials.

PLENARY

Ask one of the children to hand back the pictures of items made of wood and the piece of wood. Repeat for the other materials. Was there anything made of plastic? Why or why not?

CONSOLIDATION ACTIVITIES

Take the children on a walk around your school and see if they can identify old and new items in their environment.

46. Victorian Me

Learning Objective

Developing

Pupils can recognise and make comments about themselves and people they know in pictures of the more distant past.

Additional Skills

Fine motor: using fine motor skills to take part in dressing up activity.

Visual: recognising differences between modern and past clothing items.

Communication: commenting on pictures of themselves and others.

Resources

Interactive whiteboard (IWB)

Victorian and modern clothing for dressing up

Laminated 'past' and 'now' symbols

Tablet/camera

MAIN

- In a semicircle facing the IWB show the children the photos/video clips of Victorian children and encourage them to comment on their clothes, activities, toys, etc.

- Explain that the Victorians lived in the 'past' and that we live 'now'.

- Show the children an item of Victorian clothing and explain it's from the 'past' and place on the past symbol.

- Show the children an item of modern clothing and explain it is from 'now' and place on the 'now' symbol.

- Support the children to work together to sort the remaining clothing items.

- Support the children to choose items of Victorian clothing to dress up in and take photos of them and their classmates as they explore the clothing from the past.

PLENARY

On the IWB look at the photos as a group and support the children to recognise and comment about themselves and other people dressed in clothing from the past.

CONSOLIDATION ACTIVITIES

Look at the photos again after a few weeks or months and support the children to comment on the photos again. Have their friends changed? For example, have they got taller, have they got longer or shorter hair now?

This lesson could be repeated for other topics e.g. tasting and comparing food from Roman times and food from now.

47. Play That Video

Learning Objective

Developing

Pupils can recognise and make comments about themselves and people they know in pictures of the more distant past.

Additional Skills

Visual: noticing themselves in the past.

Attention: focusing on an activity for 7–10 minutes (or more).

Social communication: commenting on features they have noticed.

Resources

Video clip of the children in the class from 2–3 years ago

Visuals of the children as they are now and their names

MAIN

- Look back through previous class files and find a video clip of the child and their peers engaged in an activity. Ideally this will be at least 2–3 years old so that the children have changed. If a video is not available, use photos.

- Give each child in the group a visual that contains pictures of each of the people in the film as they are now, with their name underneath.

- Play the video for the children. Adults should not comment and wait for the children to respond.

- Play the video again and press pause. Ask the children who they can see in the clip; encourage them to say or point to the picture. What do they notice about the person? Are they the same or different?

- Continue watching the video and pause at key points, repeating the task.

- Leave the film on the computer or screen and allow the children to explore the video and comment on who they can see and what they are doing.

PLENARY

Tell the children that the session has ended, and ask them to turn off the video, computer and screen.

CONSOLIDATION ACTIVITIES

Find other clips of the children, or ask families to send clips in. Allow the children to have access to videos of themselves and support them to make comments on any changes that they notice.

48. Me: Past and Now

Learning Objective

Developing

Pupils can recognise some obvious distinctions between the past and the present in their own lives and communicate about these.

Additional Skills

Attention: taking part in an adult-led activity for 10 minutes.

Visual: recognising differences in photos of the past and now.

Fine motor: using pincer grip and manipulating glue stick to develop photo book.

Resources

Photos of children from their past and now with obvious distinctions e.g. in the past short hair, now long hair

Photos of familiar adults in the past and now

Laminated 'now' and 'past' symbols

Non-laminated 'now' and 'past' symbols

A5 paper

Glue sticks

MAIN

- Support the children to come to the table ready to start the activity.

- Explain that we are going to look at photos from the past and of now.

- Place the laminated 'past' and 'now' symbols on the table.

- Show the children the photo of themselves now and place it on the 'now' symbol. Then show the children a photo of them in the past; can they see any differences? Place the photo on the 'past' symbol.

- Continue to explore the 'now' and 'past' photos of the children support them to comment and to place the photos correctly onto the laminated 'now' and 'past' symbols.

PLENARY

Use the sorted photos to make a photo book of the children in the past and now. Support the children to choose a photo from the past and if possible make a comment, for example, 'In the past I was small.' Stick the photo on a piece of A5 paper and use a non-laminated 'past' symbol to label the photo. Support the children to find a 'now' photo e.g. 'Now I am big.' Stick the photo on another piece of A5 paper and use a non-laminated 'now' symbol to label the photo. Share the completed book with a classmate and/or take it home to share with family.

CONSOLIDATION ACTIVITIES

Build up the photo book across the year and add other differences about the past and now e.g. 'In the past I wore a woolly hat to school, now I wear shorts.'

49. History Dig

Learning Objective

Developing

Pupils can begin to pick historical artefacts out from collections of items.

Additional Skills

Kinaesthetic: moving around the classroom or outside to take part in the lesson.

Tactile: exploring in different sensory media.

Communication: using symbols/speech/sign to communicate to others what they have found.

Resources

Trays with different sensory media (or access to outside)

Historical artefacts for the topic e.g. for the Romans you might have pottery plates, Roman soldier hat, items of Roman clothing

Modern objects to contrast with historical artefacts e.g. to contrast with the Romans you might have plastic plates, baseball caps, items of modern clothing

MAIN

- To set up this activity, bury the historical artefacts and modern objects either in the trays with different sensory media or outside.

- Support the children to sit with a view of the IWB and show the photos/video clips of the artefacts from that time explaining these were used in the past by e.g. the Romans.

- Explain that we have to find items from the past! The way some people do this is to dig in the ground to find them as they were buried a long time ago.

- Support the children to work in pairs to dig in the trays or outside to find the historical artefacts amongst the modern items. Children can use the laminated bingo board to identify which objects are from the past and which are from 'now'.

- Adult could model handling the artefacts gently and using small brushes to wipe off the dirt, etc.

PLENARY

Once the children have found all the artefacts support them to come back to their tables/semicircle in front of the IWB. Ask each pair to share one item that they found with the class and comment on what it is and if it is from the 'past'. The children could use symbols or a pre-recorded switch to communicate to others what they found.

49. History Dig *cont.*

Interactive whiteboard (IWB)

Photos/video clips of the historical artefacts from the relevant historical topic e.g. the Romans

Tools for digging e.g. small spades

Laminated bingo board of historical artefacts to find

Whiteboard markers

CONSOLIDATION ACTIVITIES

This lesson could be repeated when exploring other topics with historical artefacts e.g. when looking at seaside holidays in the past or old and new toys.

50. Vroom

Learning Objective

Developing

Pupils begin to pick historical artefacts out from collections of items.

Additional Skills

Visual: noticing something old in a collection of items.

Attention: focusing on activity for 7–10 minutes (or more).

Social communication: taking turns and working with others.

Resources

New and old toy cars

Basket

New and old car advertising posters

New and old road signs

Pictures of new and old car interiors

MAIN

- Choose a theme that is motivating to the children; in this example we will use cars, but this can be adapted to other topics.

- Prior to the session, collate a selection of old and new toy cars.

- Place the new items in a basket with one old item.

- Show the children the basket and ask them what they can see. Give them time to explore the different objects and items.

- Place the items back in the basket. Ask a child to find an old item; wait and see what they choose.

- Replace the old item with a different one and repeat.

- See how well the children are able to recognise the old items compared to what is current.

PLENARY

Ask the children to place all the items in the basket, and count down to finish the session.

CONSOLIDATION ACTIVITIES

Place a garage out as a play experience with all of the props that you have collected; observe if the children choose the new or old items or if they mix these up.

51. Guess Who!

Learning Objective

Developing

Pupils can begin to recognise some distinctions between the past and present in other people's lives as well as their own and communicate these in simple phrases and statements.

Additional Skills

Tactile: exploring different textures in sensory media.

Kinaesthetic: moving around the classroom and returning to the front of the room.

Communication: following instructions to complete an activity.

Resources

Recent photos of children in the class/group

Photos of children in the class/group from when they were younger

Blu Tack

Trays filled with dry sensory media e.g. cornflakes, sand, flour

MAIN

- To set up this activity, Blu Tack the photos of the children as they are now onto the board/wall space with space around each photo. Bury the photos of the children when they were younger in the trays filled with sensory media and place them around the room.

- Support the children to come over to the board/wall space with the photos.

- Ask the children to identify each member of the group/class in the photos.

- Explain that these are photos of the children as they are now and buried in the trays are photos of them in the past.

- Explain that the children must carefully hunt for the photos of the children in the past, bring them to the board and match them to the photos of the children as they are now.

- Support the children to use the tools to dig in the trays, find the photos, bring them to the board and match them to the correct child.

- Encourage the children to comment as they take part in the activity on the differences between the children in the past and now.

PLENARY

Once all the 'past' photos have been found bring all the children back together at the board/wall space. Look at the photos of the children from the past and now and support the children to take turns to make comments about any differences they can see.

51. Guess Who! *cont.*

Tools for digging/cleaning
e.g. small spades,
paintbrushes for wiping
dirt from photos

CONSOLIDATION ACTIVITIES

This lesson could be repeated throughout the year as
the children grow and change.

52. From Baby to Now

Learning Objective

Developing

Pupils begin to recognise some distinctions between the past and present in other people's lives.

Additional Skills

Visual: noticing change over time.

Attention: focusing on an activity for 7–10 minutes (or more).

Communication: expressing an opinion to another person.

Resources

Pictures of yourself growing up

Large strip of paper

Pens

Visual headings (baby, child, teenager, adult)

MAIN

• Show the children pictures of yourself when you were a baby, a child, a teenager and an adult. If possible include key life events such as sporting events, graduation, wedding, new baby, first home, etc.

• Spend time looking at the pictures with the children and talking about what you are doing in them.

• Ask each child to choose their favourite picture and tell you why they like it.

• Place visual headings on a large strip of paper such as baby, child, teenager, adult.

• Ask the children to match the photo to the correct part of the timeline.

PLENARY

If you don't mind sharing your age, write the dates that the photos correspond to on the paper below the photo. Take a photo with the children on the day and print it out. Add this to the end of the timeline and write today's date.

CONSOLIDATION ACTIVITIES

For a homework project, ask families to carry out the same activity at home with members of the child's family.

53. Who Plays with This?

Learning Objective

Developing

Pupils can sort objects to given criteria.

Additional Skills

Social communication: working with a partner.

Kinaesthetic: using movement to understand that events happened in the past.

Visual: recognising differences between past and present toys.

Resources

Examples of toys from the First World War (WWI)

Examples of modern toys

A large piece of material

Laminated 'past' and 'now' symbols

Interactive whiteboard (IWB)

Photos/video clips of toys from WWI

Trays or buckets filled with dry sensory media e.g. rice, cornflakes, flour

Tools for digging

MAIN

- To set up this activity, bury a variety of modern toys and WWI toys in trays or buckets filled with dry sensory media and place around the classroom. Create two spaces by using the large piece of material as a curtain and place the 'now' symbol on one side and the 'past' symbol on the other.

- Support the children to sit with a view of the IWB and show the photos/video clips of the toys from WWI. Explain that children used these toys in the past.

- Show examples of toys from now and support the children to comment on the differences e.g. now toys light up, past toys are wood.

- Explain, 'Oh no, some toys have got lost! It is the children's job to find them and bring them back to their seats!'

- Support the child to hunt with a partner to find the modern and WWI toys in the trays/buckets filled with dry sensory media and bring them back to their seats.

PLENARY

Once all the toys have been found, encourage the children to explore them and comment on any differences. Next explain that we need to decide if the toys are from the 'past' or 'now'. With their partners, children choose an object and decide if it is from the past or now. One partner places the toy on the correct side of the curtain. If the toy is from the past ensure the children go through the curtain to place it to give the impression of going back in time!

53. Who Plays with This? *cont.*

CONSOLIDATION ACTIVITIES

This lesson could be repeated but the criteria for sorting could be changed e.g. sort by materials and then comment if past or now toys are made of plastic; sort by size and then comment if the toys from the past are bigger or smaller than the toys now.

54. Let Down Your Hair!

Learning Objective

Developing

Pupils listen to and follow stories about people and events in the past.

Additional Skills

Attention: focusing on an activity for 10 minutes or more.

Communication: answering questions, making predictions.

Fine motor: using scissors and pens.

Resources

Story set in a castle (such as Rapunzel)

Props to go with the story (old key, wig, horse, etc.)

Large cardboard boxes

Tape

Marker pens

Scissors

MAIN

- This activity uses the story of Rapunzel that is set in a castle, but you can use any story that has a castle as its location.

- Place the basket of props in front of the group; gather the children around.

- Point to the cover of the story. Can the children tell you what they can see? What do they think the story is about?

- Read the story, asking the children questions as you move through it. What is going to happen next? How do characters feel?

- Encourage children to find a prop or resource that accompanies the correct part of the story, such as a wig when they shout 'Let down your hair!'

PLENARY

Leave the book with the children and the props while you go and set up the castle role play. Use large boxes and marker pens to create the outside of the castle. Provide scissors and tape so the children can turn it into what they would like. Adult support will be needed.

CONSOLIDATION ACTIVITIES

Show the children a range of historical and new homes. Ask them if they would like to live in a castle.

55. Through the Tunnel

Learning Objective

Securing

Pupils can indicate if personal objects belong in the past or present.

Additional Skills

Gross motor: using heavy, large movements to get through the tunnel.

Kinaesthetic: moving from one area to another and maintaining attention on activity.

Social communication: playing a game with others, understanding how to win and lose with others.

Resources

Two play tunnels

Two copies of photos of the children from the past and present

Range of past and present personal objects e.g. cup/bottle, rattle/ toy the children like now, baby food/present preferred food

Four chairs

Blu Tack

Two feely bags or boxes

MAIN

- To set up this activity place the two tunnels side by side. At one end of the tunnels place two chairs. On the chairs Blu Tack the photos of the child from the past. At the other end of the tunnels place the remaining two chairs and Blu Tack the pictures of the child from the present. Place the range of personal objects in the feely bags/boxes (one for each child).

- Support the children to sit in a circle/semicircle around the tunnels.

- Ask the children in the photos to come to the front and show them the copies of their photos from past and the present.

- Then explain that the children must pull an object from the feely bag/box, decide if it is an object from their past or their present and then place the object on the correct chair. If the object is from the past they must go through the tunnel to place the object on the chair and then return to the adult to find another object. The first person to correctly sort their objects wins!

- Support the children to take part in the race; encourage other children to cheer for their friends.

- Repeat this for different members of the class and support the children to cheer for their friends and watch others take part.

PLENARY

Once all the children have taken part and have their objects from the present and the past, support them to talk about the objects with a partner or in the group e.g. which do they like best, past or present food?

55. Through the Tunnel *cont.*

CONSOLIDATION ACTIVITIES

This activity could be repeated with pictures of the children from the more recent past and objects such as their school bag from last year, etc.

56. Let's Play!

Learning Objective

Securing

Pupils indicate if personal events and objects belong in the past or present.

Additional Skills

Attention: focusing on an activity for 10 minutes or more.

Social communication: following the rules of a game.

Auditory: listening and responding to instructions.

Resources

Large image of an old street

Large image of a modern street

Access to double-sided board or two display boards

Old games (wooded quoits, bat and ball, old leather football, hopscotch, skipping rope, etc.)

New games (tablet, Connect Four, bop-it, etc.)

Basket

MAIN

- Place the large image of a street from the past on one side of a board and a modern street on the other side of the board. Place a table in front of each.

- Ask the children to identify the street from the past and the street from the present.

- Show the children the basket of games.

- Adult chooses the first game (old football) and asks the children if this is something from the past or the present.

- Go to the board/side of the street that it matches and play a game together.

- Repeat with the other games.

PLENARY

Ask the children if they liked playing the old or the new games. Ask the children to help you tidy them away.

CONSOLIDATION ACTIVITIES

Keep the basket of games available so that the children can request to play these throughout the week.

57. Today or Yesterday?

Learning Objective

Securing

Pupils can begin to use some common words/ signs or symbols to indicate the passage of time.

Additional Skills

Communication: able to recall an event and communicate this to another person.

Visual: recognising symbols and activities from weekly routine.

Auditory: responding to verbal instructions.

Resources

Laminated days of the week symbols

Laminated 'today', 'yesterday' and 'tomorrow' symbols

Photos/symbols of activities the child has taken part in from the day of this lesson and the previous day

Copies of the child's visual timetable from the day of this lesson and the previous day

MAIN

• At the end of the day, support the children to come and sit with them either at a table or a comfy spot on the carpet.

• Ask the children to identify the day of the week e.g. 'Tuesday', and then place the days of the week symbols in order in front of them.

• Say 'Yes, today is Tuesday! Yesterday was Monday.' Place the 'today' symbol under Tuesday and the 'yesterday' symbol under Monday.

• Then show the children a photo/symbol of an activity that they took part in 'today' e.g. PE, swimming, drama group, and ask the children 'Did you do swimming today or yesterday?'

• Give the children the photo/symbol and support them to place it on the correct day.

• Repeat this for all the photos/symbols of the activities the children took part in.

• If needed show the children their visual timetables from the two days to prompt their memory of when activities happened.

PLENARY

Ask the children a question e.g. 'When did you do PE?', and support them to answer using words such as 'yesterday/today'. Ask the children 'What day will it be tomorrow?' and support them to indicate e.g. 'Wednesday', by using the symbols or speech. Show the children their timetable for 'tomorrow' and discuss the activities they will be doing.

57. Today or Yesterday? *cont.*

CONSOLIDATION ACTIVITIES

Once the children are used to using terms such as 'yesterday/today/tomorrow', support them to invite a friend to come and look at their visual timetables. Support the children to talk with their friend about activities they took part in on different days.

58. My Week

Learning Objective

Securing

Pupils begin to use some common words, signs or symbols to indicate the passage of time.

Additional Skills

Attention: focusing on an activity for 10 minutes or more.

Social communication: asking and answering a question.

Fine motor: positioning pictures and sticking them down.

Resources

Digital camera/tablet for each child

Printer

Visuals (days of the week, yesterday, today, now)

Large sugar paper with 'My Week' heading

Glue

MAIN

- On a Monday morning, tell the children that they are going to record their week by taking photos on a digital camera or tablet. Take photos of your week too. Ask parents and carers if they can help by taking photos of events and activities outside of school and sending them in.

- Support the children to do this across the week.

- On Friday, print out the photos that the children have taken.

- At the start of the lesson, ask the children to sit around the table. Show them the large paper that has the heading 'My Week'. Start ordering the photos of your week and talk about what you did.

- Using symbols that have days of the week, yesterday, today and now, label the pictures.

- Give each child their pictures and symbols and headed paper so that they can create their own visual record of their week.

- Adults should support where necessary.

PLENARY

Once everyone has finished, come back as a group and each child should share their week. Adults and children should ask questions and the child will answer these.

CONSOLIDATION ACTIVITIES

This can be done a second time later in the year, and the children can compare their first week to the current one. What differences do they notice? Are the labels still correct or do they need changing?

59. Weekend Tales

Learning Objective

Securing

Pupils can recount episodes from their own past with prompts.

Additional Skills

Communication: using symbols/speech/sign in short sentences.

Social communication: sharing a story from their past with a classmate.

Attention: maintaining a short conversation with another person.

Resources

Photos/video clips from children's weekend

Symbols to prompt conversation e.g. symbols to make a sentence such as, 'I went to the cinema.'

Symbol question prompts e.g. 'Where did you go on the weekend?' 'Who did you go with?' 'Did you like what you did on the weekend?'

A4 paper

Glue sticks

Photos of children's friends

MAIN

• Support the child to choose a friend and then to come and sit at the table.

• Show the children the photos/video clips of the child's weekend.

• Prompt the child's friend to ask simple questions e.g. 'Where did you go on the weekend?', 'Who did you go with?', 'Did you like what you did at the weekend?'

• Support the child to respond to their friend's questions using symbols as a prompt or as a way to communicate a sentence to their friend.

• Then support the child to ask their friend questions about their weekend.

• A record of what their friend did could be made by sticking symbols of their friend's activity under their friend's photo on a piece of A4 paper.

PLENARY

When the class are all gathered together support the child and their friend to come to the front. Support the child and the friend to share what they learned about their respective weekends with the whole class.

CONSOLIDATION ACTIVITIES

This activity could be repeated after the school holidays as a way for the children to share their experiences with their friends.

60. Sherlock

Learning Objective

Securing

Pupils can answer simple questions about historical artefacts.

Additional Skills

Communication: using symbols/speech/sign to communicate ideas.

Visual: using observation skills to answer simple questions.

Attention: maintaining concentration and attention on an activity for 15 minutes.

Resources

Familiar historical artefacts e.g. objects used in previous lessons to explore the topic, such as the Romans, seaside holidays from the past, the Tudors

Matching objects from the present e.g. if exploring items from the Romans, have a plastic jug/plate to contrast with a pottery jug/plate

Handheld child-friendly magnifying glass

MAIN

- To set up this activity place the historical artefacts and the objects from the present on a table top all mixed up.
- Support the children to come over to the table and explain that we are going to play detective.
- Model choosing an item and using the magnifying glass to inspect it. Comment on the object e.g. 'I see it looks old. I see it is made from pottery. I think the plate is Roman.'
- Then place the 'Roman plate' in the box labelled 'Roman'.
- Support the children to do the same with other objects and artefacts.
- Ask the children simple questions such as, 'Is the bucket plastic or wood?', 'Is the cup metal or plastic?', 'Does the toy need batteries?' (The questions will depend on the topic being explored.)
- Support the children to use the magnifying glass to explore the artefact closely and to answer the questions using symbols/speech or sign.

PLENARY

Once all the objects and artefacts have been explored and sorted, ask the children to place them all back on the table. Support each child to choose a friend to come over to the table to play 'Sherlock' and encourage the child to ask their friend the simple questions. Alternatively, the child and friend could explore the objects and artefacts together while the adult asks the questions.

60. Sherlock *cont.*

Two boxes: one labelled with the history topic e.g. Roman, Tudor, and one labelled 'now/present'

Laminated symbols with possible answers to the simple questions if needed to support the children's communication

CONSOLIDATION ACTIVITIES

Use the magnifying glasses in other topics and in play as a way to support the children to explore objects more closely. Ask the children simple questions about other objects such as mini-beasts, different materials, various geographical signs, etc.

61. On Stage

Learning Objective

Securing

Pupils recount some details from historical events with prompts.

Additional Skills

Attention: focusing on an activity for more than 10 minutes.

Social communication: speaking clearly to maintain a short conversation with others.

Fine motor: using scissors, pens, etc.

Resources

Story of Romulus and Remus

Strips of paper

Marker pens

Card

Scissors

String

Tablet device to record

MAIN

- Following on from the 'How Rome Was Built' activity, read the story of Romulus and Remus to the children.

- Ask the children to retell you parts of the story. Write what they say on strips of paper.

- Order the story together.

- Read it aloud to the children. Are any parts missing?

- Ask the children questions such as, 'Who found the babies?', 'Who was the first king of Rome?'

- Then everyone chooses a character and makes a mask (Romulus, Remus, babies, wolf, shepherd).

- As a group, act out the story of Romulus and Remus.

PLENARY

Film the children acting, and watch this back together. Ask the children what their favourite part was and if they could add anything for next time.

CONSOLIDATION ACTIVITIES

Place a basket of Roman costumes for props in the reading corner with a selection of fiction and non-fiction books about Rome so the children can explore the stories from that era.

LANGUAGES

62. Drum Circle

Learning Objective

Emerging

Pupils can attempt to repeat, copy or imitate some sounds heard in the target language.

Additional Skills

Social communication: taking part in a small group activity.

Auditory: listening to sounds and attempting to imitate.

Gross motor: using a large arm movement for banging the drum.

Resources

A drum per child

A drum for the lead adult

MAIN

- Support 4–5 children to sit in a small circle.
- Give each child a drum.
- Say a short word or sound in the target language and bang out the syllables on the drum.
- Support the children to imitate the word and sound and banging on the drum.
- Repeat this for different sounds and words in the target language.

PLENARY

Each child takes a turn making a word or sound and banging the drum with the others in the group, then imitating them.

CONSOLIDATION ACTIVITIES

This activity could be used as a hello session in the target language at the start of a lesson: the adult bangs 'hello' in the target language with the child's name and the child then attempts to imitate the word and drumbeat back to the adult.

63. Sing It Differently

Learning Objective

Emerging

Pupils attempt to repeat or copy or imitate some sounds heard in the target language.

Additional Skills

Auditory: noticing a familiar tune.

Attention: focusing on an activity for 3–5 minutes (or more).

Social communication: joining in with a familiar adult.

Resources

Access to a computer or music and speakers

The words to a familiar nursery rhyme in chosen target language

MAIN

- Play the music from a familiar nursery rhyme to the children e.g. 'Twinkle Twinkle Little Star', to gain their attention.

- Then, either using an online video, or a confident adult, sing the song in the target language, using actions where possible.

- Repeat this a few times and then say to the children that it is their turn. Encourage them to join in where possible.

PLENARY

Sing the song together one last time, all adults in the room to join in. Then count the children down, '5, 4, 3, 2, 1, singing has finished.'

CONSOLIDATION ACTIVITIES

In circle time that week, play the same song each day so that the new words become more familiar to the children.

64. Me for My Turn!

Learning Objective

Emerging

Pupils can perform familiar or simple gestures on request using repetition, sign or gesture as prompts.

Additional Skills

Communication: indicating their desire for a turn.

Social communication: waiting for a turn as part of a small group.

Attention: maintaining attention on an adult-led activity for 3–5 minutes (or more).

Resources

Props to represent two songs in target language

MAIN

- Support 3–4 children to sit in a semicircle ready to learn.

- Model using their whole hand facing toward them and touching their chest, saying 'me' in the target language and then choosing a prop that prompts a song that the group sings in the target language.

- Then encourage/support the child to gesture 'me', possibly imitating the sound in the target language.

- Then support the child to make a choice from the two props to prompt the child's chosen song in the target language.

- Repeat this for every child in the small group.

PLENARY

Sing a goodbye song in the target language that has a few simple gestures, such as waving, and encourage the child to join in with the gestures at the appropriate time in the song.

CONSOLIDATION ACTIVITIES

In other sessions, games and activities across the day support the children to indicate 'me' for a turn using the physical gesture of touching their chest with the front of their whole hand. This may not necessarily have to happen in the target language.

65. Simon Dit...

Learning Objective

Emerging

Pupils may perform familiar or simple action on request using repetition, sign or gesture as prompts.

Additional Skills

Auditory: beginning to recognise new words.

Attention: focusing on an activity for 3–5 minutes (or more).

Visual: using pictures to help understand instructions.

Resources

Body parts printed on A4 paper with the target language word

MAIN

- This game is Simon Says (adult does an action, children copy) using the chosen target language.

- Work with a small group of children and show them pictures of body parts. Ask the children to touch their body part as the picture is shown (for example, picture of an ear, touch the ear). Have the target language words written on the card also, and adult to say that word.

- Start the game by using the sentence 'Simon says point to...' in the target language as the word is said for the children; show them the picture card so that you are reinforcing the language.

- Other adults in the group model touch the body part also.

- Repeat so that the children become familiar with the game and the target language.

PLENARY

Quick fire! Show each of the cards and see if the children can move quickly through the different body parts. Count the group down and finish the activity.

CONSOLIDATION ACTIVITIES

Play this across the week; you can ask the children if they would like to take a turn at holding the cards up for the rest of the group.

66. Action Me!

Learning Objective

Emerging

Pupils can listen and respond to familiar rhymes and songs in a foreign language.

Additional Skills

Auditory: listen and respond to a song in a foreign language.

Kinaesthetic: respond physically to a song in a foreign language.

Visual: imitate and copy actions performed by another person.

Resources

Props to represent action songs in target language

MAIN

- To set up this activity select one or two familiar action songs that can be sung in the target language e.g. 'Head Shoulders Knees and Toes' and 'The Wheels on the Bus' and choose appropriate props that represent each song.

- Support 3–4 children to sit in a semicircle ready to learn.

- Show the children a prop for the action song and then model the song in the target language, touching e.g. head, shoulders, knees and toes respectively and naming them in target language.

- Encourage and support the children to join in with actions when sung in target language.

- Introduce another song in the same way.

- When the children are familiar with both songs, offer them a choice of songs by showing them the props and supporting them to make a choice.

PLENARY

Children remain in the group and join in the song as each of their classmates makes a choice.

CONSOLIDATION ACTIVITIES

Have the props for the songs available in e.g. the book corner and show the children that they are there. If at any point children independently choose to explore one of the props the adult can sing the corresponding song with them in the target language.

67. Play It with Me

Learning Objective

Emerging

Pupils listen and may respond to familiar rhymes and songs in a foreign language.

Additional Skills

Auditory: listening to familiar tunes.

Attention: focusing on an activity for 3–5 minutes (or more).

Social communication: taking a turn.

Fine motor: using sticks and beaters to play instruments.

Resources

Pre-prepared PowerPoint with images of favourite songs linking to the song in the target language

Access to a computer

Box of instruments

MAIN

- Prior to the lesson, create a song choice PowerPoint board with images connected to the children's favourite classroom songs that link through to a version in the target language.

- Place the chairs in a semicircle around the board with a box of instruments in the centre. Ask all the children to join you.

- Taking turns, ask the children to choose a song from the board, take their seat and use their instrument to join in.

- At the end of a song, all children pass their instrument to a friend and take a new one.

- It is then the next child's turn to choose a song from the board.

PLENARY

Play a goodbye song in the target language. Ask all the children to put their instruments back in the box and count down the lesson so that everyone knows it has finished.

CONSOLIDATION ACTIVITIES

Place some target language songs on a tablet with headphones and have this as a choice that the children can make through the day.

68. Colour Hunt

Learning Objective

Emerging

Pupils can attempt one or two words in the target language in response to a familiar phrase.

Additional Skills

Communication: respond appropriately to a simple spoken phrase.

Visual: able to recognise and match colours.

Tactile: experience different sensory media.

Resources

A large coloured dot with name of the colour in target language written underneath

Items/objects in that colour

Sensory bin (a bucket or box filled with dry sensory media such as rice)

MAIN

- To set up this activity, bury all the coloured items/objects in the sensory bin and place the large coloured dot on a table next to the sensory bin.

- Support the children to come over to the sensory bin.

- Show the children the coloured dot and name the colour in the target language.

- Then model hunting in the sensory bin for an object, matching it to the coloured dot and saying the name of the colour in the target language.

- Support the children to do the same until all the objects have been found.

- Encourage the children each time to say the name of the colour in the target language in response to the phrase 'What colour is it?'

- Introduce a second colour in the same way.

- When the children are able to recognise and understand the two colours, place the two large coloured dots side by side and all the coloured items into one sensory bin.

- Then support the children to find a coloured object, match it to the correct colour and attempt to say the name of the colour in the target language in response to the phrase 'What colour is it?'

PLENARY

Ask children 'Where is (colour)?' and support the children to indicate the colour through gesture. Then ask the children to place all the coloured objects back in the sensory bin, saying the colour in the target language for each object.

68. Colour Hunt *cont.*

CONSOLIDATION ACTIVITIES

Across the day in other sessions and in different environments encourage the children to identify the familiar colour in the target language e.g. if the colour introduced was green when in the playground point to a bush and ask the children 'What colour is it?' and encourage their response.

69. Hello, Bonjour, Ciao

Learning Objective

Emerging

Pupils attempt one or two words in the target language in response to cues in a song or familiar phrase.

Additional Skills

Auditory: listening to others' greetings.

Attention: focusing on an activity for 5–7 minutes (or more).

Social communication: taking a turn.

Resources

'Hello' in English, laminated

'Hello' in target language, laminated

Board

MAIN

• If you are learning one target language, place the symbol and word for 'hello' in that language on a board along with 'hello' in English. If you are learning a few ways to greet people, then place all of the languages on the board.

• During a greeting session, place the board with the different 'hello' words in front of the group. Sing the song 'Hello hello hello, hello hello hello, hello hello hello, oh it's good to see you here!'; ask the children to greet you back by choosing either English or the target language hello word from the board. Encourage them to say it aloud if they can.

• Ask a child to go around the group saying hello in the chosen language and shaking hands or giving a high five to each of the other children.

• Repeat with all children in the group.

PLENARY

Complete your greetings session in the typical manner, either looking at the weather or news reports of the day. Then ask the children to check their timetables.

CONSOLIDATION ACTIVITIES

Learn a new greetings song in the target language and introduce that to your circle time. Singing daily can help the children to learn a new set of lyrics.

70. Stop! Go!

Learning Objective

Emerging

Pupils can respond to simple instructions about familiar experiences.

Additional Skills

Auditory: responding appropriately to verbal/visual instruction.

Kinaesthetic: moving body in response to different action instructions.

Social communication: taking part in activity as part of a small group.

Resources

Large pocket dice with different action symbols labelled in target language in each pocket

Large 'Stop' and 'Go' symbols and words in target language

MAIN

- Support the children to sit in a semicircle ready to learn.

- Ask a model adult/child to come to the front to model the game.

- Model adult/child rolls the large pocket dice and names the action shown in the target language (if possible).

- Everybody stands up and joins in the action.

- Lead adult uses the laminate 'Stop' and 'Go' symbols as well as the verbal instruction in the target language; model adult/child responds to instructions.

- Support every child in the group to take a turn rolling the dice, labelling the action in the target language, and then the whole group taking part in the action and responding to 'stop' and 'go' instructions in the target language.

PLENARY

Once everyone has had a turn, count down '5, 4, 3, 2, 1, finished' in the target language, along with using gestures, to indicate the lesson has finished.

CONSOLIDATION ACTIVITIES

This lesson could be taken outside and used in the playground at lunch or playtimes by the children.

71. Teddy Wants...

Learning Objective

Emerging

Pupils can respond to simple requests about familiar experiences.

Additional Skills

Communication: responding appropriately to a request made by another person.

Social communication: taking part in a simple role play game.

Auditory: processing a request made by another person.

Resources

A teddy

Familiar food items for a picnic (real or pretend)

Box/plate for the food items

Symbols for each food item, labelled in the target language

MAIN

- Support the children to come and sit at the table for a picnic with teddy.

- Show the children each food item, verbally label it in the target language and then match it to the symbol.

- Place the food items next to the children and explain teddy is hungry and wants to ask for some food.

- Pretend to be the teddy making requests for food items in the target language e.g. 'Can teddy have cake?'

- Children may need initial support from a second adult to find the food item and give it to teddy to eat.

PLENARY

Once teddy has requested all the food items in the target language, support the children to request food items using speech or symbols, ideally in the target language.

CONSOLIDATION ACTIVITIES

At snack or lunchtimes adult could make requests from the children for different foods in the target language.

72. Good, Bad, OK

Learning Objective

Emerging

Pupils respond to simple questions about familiar events.

Additional Skills

Auditory: listening to others' responses.

Attention: focusing on an activity for 5–7 minutes (or more).

Social communication: taking a turn.

Visual: matching picture to correct feeling.

Resources

Laminated board with three columns and the headings and visuals for 'good', 'bad' and 'OK' (smiley face, sad face and thumbs up)

Small laminated pictures of each person (adult and child) in the group

Whiteboard pen

MAIN

- Focusing on the target language for the class, ensure that the adults are all aware of the translation for the key question, 'How are you today?' and the responses for 'good', 'bad' and 'OK'.

- Place the board with the smiley face, sad face and thumbs up in front of the children.

- Sitting in a circle, give each of the children a picture of themselves, and ensure that the adults have pictures too, so that they can join in.

- Ask a child, 'How are you today?' in the target language, and wait for them to respond by verbally speaking, facial expression or pointing to one of the visuals on the board. Ask them to place their face in the column that matches their emotion.

- Repeat for the rest of the group.

PLENARY

Once everyone has their faces on the board, ask in the target language, 'How many people feel good/bad/OK?' Ask a child to come with the adult supporting and count numbers in the target language. Have a whiteboard pen ready so the number can be written at the bottom of the column.

CONSOLIDATION ACTIVITIES

Play number songs or feelings songs in the target language at points during the day, so that the children become familiar with hearing another language.

73. Roll It, Move It

Learning Objective

Emerging

Pupils' responses may be through vocalisation, sign or gesture.

Additional Skills

Auditory: listening to two instructions.

Attention: focusing on an activity for 5–7 minutes (or more).

Social communication: taking a turn as part of a small group.

Visual: matching picture to correct action.

Kinaesthetic: moving body in a variety of ways.

Resources

Two pocket dice

Cards to fit in the dice (one set of six with action pictures and target language, one set of six with numbers)

Access to relaxing music

MAIN

- Stand in a circle, ideally in the hall or playground, or at least clear some space in the classroom.

- Show the children the dice that you have and the pictures and words that are on it.

- Model rolling the dice. Read out the action word in the target language and point to the picture of the action. Everyone in the group should do the action.

- Then add the second dice with numbers. Model rolling both dice. Look at the number, read this out in the target language, and then add this to the action; everyone joins in. Count in the target language as you go. This should be numbers either 0–5 or 1–6.

- Offer the dice to a child in the group so that they can roll them and work out how many of the actions they need to tell the group to do. Support with giving the number and action in the target language.

- Repeat with the whole group.

PLENARY

Put some relaxing music on after a busy session; encourage the children to sit and breathe deeply. After 2 minutes count down from 5 to 0 and finish the activity.

CONSOLIDATION ACTIVITIES

Put the dice in the choosing box, toy box or out on the playground so that the children can play this game with adults and peers. If numbers are a strength, change the number dice to counting in twos or fives.

74. Ola!

Learning Objective

Developing

Pupils can respond to others in a group.

Additional Skills

Social communication: initiating an interaction with a classmate.

Communication: making a choice.

Attention: maintaining focus and attention for 5–8 minutes.

Resources

Two choice boards

Laminated photos of children in small group with Velcro on the back

Laminated symbols of actions labelled in target language e.g. high five, tickle, shake hands, with Velcro on the back

MAIN

- To set up this activity place all the laminated photos of the children in the small group on one of the choice boards. Place all the laminated action symbols onto another choice board.

- Support a group of 5–6 children to sit in a semicircle ready to learn.

- Model choosing a child from the pictures, going to them and saying 'hello' in the target language. Encourage the child to respond by imitating the word.

- Then offer the child the choice board with action symbols and support the child to choose an action.

- Label the action in the target language and then do the action with the child.

- Then pass the picture choice board to the child who repeats this process with a classmate.

- Repeat this process until all the children have had a chance to choose a friend and to respond to their friend's greeting.

PLENARY

Support the children to go around the group collecting up the photos of their friends and place them back on the choice board. Adult, along with children if possible, counts down '5, 4, 3, 2, 1, finished' and shows the children the next activity on the timetable.

CONSOLIDATION ACTIVITIES

Use the picture choice board to support the children to choose a friend for activities across the day and support the children to greet their friend in similar ways learned in this lesson.

75. Language Whispers

Learning Objective

Developing

Pupils respond to others in a group.

Additional Skills

Auditory: listening to noun.

Attention: focusing on an activity for 10–15 minutes (or more).

Social communication: taking a turn, understanding rules.

Kinaesthetic: moving body in a variety of ways.

Resources

Canvas bag

Pictures of animals with the target language underneath

MAIN

- Sitting on chairs in a circle, place the bag of animal pictures in the centre of the group.

- Lead adult takes out each animal. Practise saying the name of each of the animals in the target language.

- At the beginning of the activity have only 3–4 animals in the bag; this can be increased as the children become more familiar with the names of more animals.

- Tell the children that you are all going to play 'Chinese Whispers', where you need to whisper a word to the next person.

- Model taking an animal from the bag, look at it and then sit on it. Whisper the name of the animal in the target language to the person sitting next to you. That person whispers to the next person and so on.

- The last person in the group to hear the whisper has to act out the animal and say the word. The first person, in this case the adult, shows the group the card and they all work out if they got it right or wrong.

- Repeat.

PLENARY

Once you have been playing the game for around 10–15 minutes, all stand up. Adult pulls an animal from the bag and all act this out together for a movement break. Count down the children and tell them the lesson has finished.

CONSOLIDATION ACTIVITIES

Place a set of small world animals into a bag. The children can put their hand in, pull one out and try to match it to a name card of the animal name in the target language.

76. Rojo, Naranja, Verde

Learning Objective

Developing

Pupils respond to others in a group.

Additional Skills

Auditory: listening to instructions.

Attention: focusing on an activity for 10–15 minutes (or more).

Social communication: taking a turn, understanding rules.

Kinaesthetic: moving body in a variety of ways.

Resources

Access to music to warm up and cool down

Red, green and orange A4 cards, laminated

MAIN

- Out on the playground or in the hall, all the children in the group spread out.

- Warm up by playing some music and running, jumping and stretching.

- Teach the children the rules of the traffic light game. Show everyone the green card and say 'green' in the target language. All the children need to run when the light is green. Show the orange card and say 'orange' in target language; everyone needs to walk. The last card is red; say 'red' in target language and everyone needs to stop.

- Practise by holding up the cards and have other adults in the group support the different actions.

- Choose a child to come and be the traffic controller. They hold up the cards and where possible say the colour in the target language (an adult can support if needed).

- Repeat so that all children in the group take a turn.

PLENARY

Cool down by playing some relaxing music and stretching the body and finish with some deep breaths.

CONSOLIDATION ACTIVITIES

In the playground, place the coloured cards in an accessible place so the children can play the new game they have learned.

77. I Want...

Learning Objective

Developing

Pupils' attempts to communicate in the target language may rely heavily upon repetition and gesture to enhance meaning.

Additional Skills

Communication: using gesture to communicate a choice between two objects.

Fine motor: using pincer grip to select and pick up a symbol.

Resources

Range of really motivating toys for the children

Some non-motivating items

Symbols/photos of objects labelled in target language

Box for tidying up

MAIN

- Present the children with a motivating and a non-motivating item and ask, 'What do you want?'
- Verbally label the items in the target language and place photo/symbol in front of each object.
- Encourage the children to indicate which object they want through speech by imitating the target language and/or gesture (pointing, etc.) and then taking the photo/symbol and handing it to the adult.
- Again verbally label the chosen object in the target language and hand it to the children to explore for a short period.
- Repeat this for other motivating and non-motivating items.

PLENARY

Ask the children to tidy the items away by verbally labelling them in the target language and showing the children the photo/symbol of the items and indicating placing them back in the box.

CONSOLIDATION ACTIVITIES

At playtimes or during free choice times have the familiar motivating and non-motivating items available for the children to explore and encourage them to name the items in the target and native language.

78. Tasty Talking

Learning Objective

Developing

Pupils can communicate positives and negatives in the target language in response to simple questions.

Additional Skills

Tactile: exploring and tasting new foods.

Communication: using speech/symbol/ sign to communicate a preference.

Social communication: taking turns as part of a small group.

Resources

Food from target language country

Laminated 'like' and 'don't like' symbols labelled in target language

Laminated symbols of the food for tasting labelled in target language

Large piece of paper divided into two columns labelled 'Like' and 'Don't like' in target language and with symbols

MAIN

- Support 3–5 children to come and sit at the table ready to learn.

- Explain that today we are going to taste some new food from (country) where they speak (target language).

- Select a food item, show it to the children, verbally label it in the target language, show the children the corresponding symbol and then model tasting the food.

- Model using the 'Like' symbol to indicate they like the food.

- Then offer the food to each child in turn, each time verbally labelling it in the target language.

- Support the children to express whether they liked or did not like the food item using the symbols and attempting the words in the target language in response to the question 'Do you like or not like the (food in target language)?'

PLENARY

After tasting all the foods, show the children the large piece of paper divided into two columns. As a group sort the food symbols into the 'Like' and 'Don't like' columns, each time encouraging the children to use the target language to label the food and express their preference.

CONSOLIDATION ACTIVITIES

This lesson could be repeated with objects/items other than food presented to the children so that they can express their preference using the target language supported by symbols.

79. Do You Like Spinach Ice Cream?

Learning Objective

Developing

Pupils communicate positives and negatives in the target language in response to simple questions.

Additional Skills

Auditory: listening to instructions.

Attention: focusing on an activity for 10–15 minutes (or more).

Social communication: taking a turn, understanding rules.

Kinaesthetic: running and moving.

Resources

A4 cards with a food item on each (around 20)

A4 poster with 'Yes' in target language

A4 poster with 'No' in target language

MAIN

- Before the lesson, prepare some food cards, such as banana, spinach, peanut butter, chocolate milkshake, tomato ketchup: about 20 altogether.

- Place posters with 'Yes' and 'No' in the target language, one at each end of the room.

- Gather the group in the centre of the room, show them the posters and read the words in the target language; use thumbs up and thumbs down to support the yes and no element.

- Show the group a food item; ask them do they like it? The children need to respond yes or no by running to one end of the room or the other.

- Once they have had a few turns with single food items, put two together, such as spinach ice cream; do the children like that?

- Ask the children one by one to take a turn and to create funny food combinations for their group.

PLENARY

Cool down by playing some relaxing music and stretching the body and finish with some deep breaths.

CONSOLIDATION ACTIVITIES

Use this activity to make a tally chart of the foods that children like and don't like; encourage them to make sets of five when drawing the tally marks.

80. Action Match!

Learning Objective

Developing

Pupils can match and select symbols for familiar actions presented in the target language.

Additional Skills

Visual: able to recognise and match two symbols that look the same.

Social communication: able to take a turn as part of a small group.

Kinaesthetic: moving body in a specific way e.g. star jump.

Resources

Feely bag

Two sets of laminated action symbols labelled in target language

Choice board

Blu Tack

MAIN

- To set up this activity place one set of the laminated action symbols in the feely bag and the other set on the choice board.

- Support 3–5 children to come to the carpet or large space ready to learn.

- Show the group the choice board and name each action symbol in the target language, encouraging the children to imitate the word.

- Attach the choice board to a solid surface such as the wall using the Blu Tack.

- Choose a child, present them with the feely bag, and sing the song (to the tune of 'Jingle Bells'): 'Feely bag, feely bag, what's inside the feely bag? Put your hand in, feel about, when you're ready pull something out!'

- The child pulls out an action symbol, runs to match it to the choice board and then performs the action for the group.

- Repeat this until every child has had a turn.

PLENARY

Once all the symbols have been matched, ask each child in turn to find an action symbol in the target language from the choice board and place it in the feely bag ready for the next session.

CONSOLIDATION ACTIVITIES

This lesson could be taken on the playground and used by the children at playtimes. The adult can support by repeatedly labelling the actions in the target language.

81. See It, Find It

Learning Objective

Developing

Pupils match and select symbols for familiar objects presented in the target language.

Additional Skills

Visual: searching out objects.

Attention: focusing on an activity for 10–15 minutes (or more).

Social communication: negotiating with others.

Kinaesthetic: moving around the classroom.

Resources

Picture cards (everyday classroom items with the word written in the target language)

MAIN

- Place four of the object cards face down in front of each child.

- Ask the children to turn the first card over. It will have the picture of the object and the word in the target language. Ask the children to go and find the item in the room and match it to the picture.

- Repeat for the remaining three cards.

- At the end of the hunt, each child shares with the group what they have found, showing the picture card and attempting to say the word in the target language if able. Adults support with the vocabulary where necessary.

PLENARY

Ask the children to return to the objects where they found them and hand the cards back to the lead adult. Count down '5, 4, 3, 2, 1, finished' to finish the activity.

CONSOLIDATION ACTIVITIES

Hand the cards out with Blu Tack and allow the children to 'label' the classroom with the pictures and target language vocabulary.

82. Release Me!

Learning Objective

Developing

Pupils can introduce themselves by name in response to a question in the target language.

Additional Skills

Kinaesthetic: stopping and resuming movement in response to interaction with a classmate.

Social communication: taking part in a game with classmates.

Auditory: listening and responding appropriately to questions posed by others.

Resources

Large space for running around in

Laminated symbol sentence: 'What is your name?' labelled in target language

MAIN

- Before the main part of this lesson, spend some time with the children introducing the phrase 'What is your name?' in the target language and the correct response, that is, saying your name.

- Choose one or two children to be 'It' (depending on class size).

- The other children run around and 'It' has to touch them gently, or 'tag' them, to freeze their classmates.

- The children who are not 'tagged' can unfreeze their friends by asking them 'What is your name?' in the target language and the frozen child must respond with their name before they can resume running around again.

- Some children may need to use the laminated symbol sentence to ask their friends 'What is your name?' in the target language to unfreeze them.

PLENARY

Once all the children are frozen the adult asks the whole group 'What is your name?' and everyone responds with their name to reset the game and start again with different children as 'It'.

CONSOLIDATION ACTIVITIES

Support the children to play this game on the playground; introduce other people in the school to the phrase and correct response.

83. Are You at School Today?

Learning Objective

Developing

Pupils introduce themselves by name in response to a question in the target language.

Additional Skills

Auditory: listening to each other.

Attention: focusing on an activity for 10–15 minutes (or more).

Social communication: greeting others appropriately.

Resources

None

MAIN

- Set this activity up during a morning or afternoon registration period.

- Work down the list of group/class members, asking each one in the target language, 'Are you in school today?'

- The child responds with 'yes' in the target language if they are at school.

- They then stand up and go around the group and greet (shake hands, high five, eye contact, whatever is appropriate) the other children in the group, saying 'good morning/afternoon' in the target language.

- Repeat with the remaining children in the group.

PLENARY

Show the timetable for what is next and count the group down to indicate that registration has finished.

CONSOLIDATION ACTIVITIES

As the children become confident greeting each other, begin to introduce a question that they can ask, such as, 'How do you feel today?' Ensure that the children have the visuals or the language needed to respond to any new questions.

84. aMAZEing Directions

Learning Objective

Developing

Pupils can contribute to using the target language for a purpose.

Additional Skills

Communication: using symbol/speech/sign to direct another person's movements.

Social communication: working as part of small group.

Visual: awareness of simple directional instructions.

Resources

Playground chalk

'Treasure'

Laminated symbols of basic directions labelled in target language e.g. back, forwards, left, right

MAIN

- To set up this activity, draw, possibly with the support of the child, a simple maze on the playground floor using the chalk and place the 'treasure' at the end of the maze.

- Support the child along with two classmates to come over to the drawn maze.

- Introduce the basic direction symbols, verbally label them in the target language and model them.

- Support the children to use the symbols and speech in target language to direct each other around the simple maze to retrieve the treasure!

- Repeat so that everyone has a turn giving and receiving instructions.

PLENARY

Once everyone has had a turn see if the children can direct each other back to the classroom using the symbols and direction words in the target language.

CONSOLIDATION ACTIVITIES

At different points across the day and during times such as playtimes support each child to choose a friend and support them to use the symbols to direct each other to different areas e.g. their seat, the slide.

85. Translate Me

Learning Objective

Developing

Pupils contribute to using the target language for a purpose.

Additional Skills

Auditory: listening to target language.

Attention: focusing on an activity for 10–15 minutes (or more).

Fine motor: using a keyboard and mouse.

Resources

Access to a computer with the Internet

Visual instructions for loading an Internet-based translation program

Animal picture cards with English word and space for target language (four per child)

Set of small world animals that match the picture cards

MAIN

- If this is the first time the lesson has been presented to the child, work on a one-to-one basis. Sit in front of the computer and encourage the child to log on and open a web browser.

- Show the child the first visual instruction, 'type Google', with a picture of what this looks like.

- Once in Google, show the second visual instruction, 'type Google translate'. Give the child time to complete this instruction.

- Present the third visual instruction 'set English as language 1 and (target language) as translation'. An adult may need to support the child with any of the previous three instructions as necessary.

- Give the child the four animal cards with the word in English at the top of the picture and a blank line underneath. Give them a pen/pencil to write the word in the target language once they have used the translation program.

- If the child is able, leave them to type in the animal words in English; only offer support if needed. Press the sound button to hear the word in the target language.

- Child writes the target language name of the animal on the correct picture.

- Repeat for all animals.

- Other children in the group should have a different set of animals each for this activity.

PLENARY

Once all the children have had a turn at translating the animal names, place all the small world animals out in front of the group and ask the children to use their images and translations to label the animals.

85. Translate Me *cont.*

CONSOLIDATION ACTIVITIES

If you set up a small world play scenario, leave a tablet computer and blank labels and pens near to it so that the children can find the name of the objects that they are playing with in the target language.

86. Numeral Naming

Learning Objective

Developing

Pupils can listen, attend to and follow familiar interactions in target language.

Additional Skills

Communication: choosing between two photos/symbols.

Tactile: experiencing different messy media.

Social communication: waiting for a turn as part of a small group.

Resources

Water spray/bubbles/ shaving foam

Laminated photos/ symbols of messy media labelled in target language

Choice board

Laminated number symbol cards '1' and '2', labelled in target language

MAIN

- Support a small group of children to come and sit in a semicircle.

- Show the children each symbol of messy media; verbally label it in the target language and place it on the choice board.

- Show the children the numeral symbols and label the numbers in the target language.

- Present a child with the messy media choice board; support them to choose e.g. the water spray and then to choose a numeral, 1 or 2, and attempt to say it in the target language.

- Child then receives e.g. one or two sprays of the water spray depending on their choice.

- Repeat this for all the children in the group.

- Child waits for their turn and learns how to interact with the activity by watching their peers.

PLENARY

Repeat the lesson again but this time with the children taking it in turns to play the role of the adult to encourage peer-to-peer interactions in the target language.

CONSOLIDATION ACTIVITIES

Place the resources for this game in a zip-lock bag or other container and keep it in an accessible place such as the library corner. Encourage the child to independently use the resources to interact with a chosen friend at appropriate times during the day.

87. Story Time

Learning Objective

Developing

Pupils listen, attend and follow familiar interactions in the target language.

Additional Skills

Auditory: listening to target language.

Attention: focusing on an activity for 10–15 minutes (or more).

Social communication: sharing items appropriately with others.

Resources

Familiar classroom book in target language

Canvas bag

Real props to accompany the story (or laminated pictures)

MAIN

- Choosing a familiar classroom story, all sit in the book corner with the bag of props in the middle of the group.

- Begin to read the story in the target language, pointing to the pictures to alert the children to the key characters or plot line.

- As each character is introduced, ask a child to look in the prop bag, find the matching item and pass this around the group.

- Continue reading the story and exploring the props.

PLENARY

Once the story has finished, ask the children one by one to put their prop back in the bag and count down the group to indicate the session has finished.

CONSOLIDATION ACTIVITIES

Place the book in English and the book in the target language in the book corner with the props so that the children can explore each of the items.

88. Sensational Story Telling

Learning Objective

Securing

Pupils can listen attentively and know that the target language conveys meaning.

Additional Skills

Attention: maintain attention on an adult-led activity for 15 minutes.

Communication: make a choice between different props to indicate meaning.

Auditory: able to respond appropriately to certain points in a familiar story.

Resources

A short story about the weather written in target language supported by symbols/pictures e.g. In summer the sun shines. In autumn the wind blows. In winter the snow flurries. In spring the rain falls.

Props to match weather e.g. sunglasses for sun, handheld fan for wind, shaving foam for snow, water spray for rain.

MAIN

- Support a small group of children to come and sit in a semicircle ready to learn.

- Read the story to the children in the target language using the relevant props at the correct point in the story.

- Then read the story again. This time at the point in the story when a prop is needed, present a child with two props and support them to choose the prop most relevant to that point in the story e.g. the shaving foam for snow.

- Child then matches the prop to the page in the storybook and uses the prop with their friends, possibly imitating the word in the target language e.g. 'snow!'

PLENARY

At the end of the story support each child to choose their favourite prop from a selection presented to them in the target language. After a short time exploring the prop, count down '5, 4, 3, 2, 1, finished' in the target language. Name each prop in the target language and indicate to the child holding that prop to hand it back to you.

CONSOLIDATION ACTIVITIES

Other concepts such as colours, animals, foods, etc. could be introduced in the target language using short sensory stories with corresponding props.

89. Bingo!

Learning Objective

Securing

Pupils listen attentively and know that the target language conveys meaning.

Additional Skills

Auditory: listening to target language.

Attention: focusing on an activity for 15 minutes (or more).

Fine motor: moving counters.

Social communication: following the rules of a game.

Resources

Bingo boards (pictures of familiar items)

Counters

Images of each of the items

Bag

MAIN

- Place the bingo boards in front of each child who is joining the session and give them a counter for each square of the board. Have the words in the target language ready to read out and the images to show the children if they need visual support.

- Model two goes for the whole group; pull out an image from the bag, do not show the children yet, and say the word in the target language. Repeat it a few times. Encourage the children to listen and place a counter over the image if they have it.

- If they are still stuck, show them the image to support playing the game.

- After the two practice turns, take the counters off and start again.

- Repeat the turns until someone has bingo!

- Swap the boards around if the children are keen to play again.

PLENARY

Count down '5, 4, 3, 2, 1' and place all the counters and bingo boards in the tidy-up box.

CONSOLIDATION ACTIVITIES

Create a pack of the bingo boards so that the children can play this by themselves during a choosing time.

90. Roll-a-Command

Learning Objective

Securing

Pupils can understand one or two simple classroom commands in the target language.

Additional Skills

Gross motor: making large movements in response to verbal/visual instructions.

Social communication: taking part in an activity as part of a large group.

Auditory: responding appropriately to verbal instructions.

Resources

Large laminated 'Sit' and 'Stand' symbols labelled in the target language

Large pocket dice (with sit and stand symbols in the pocket)

MAIN

- Support the children to come and sit in a circle on the carpet.
- Show the children the large pocket dice; model rolling it and reading the command e.g. 'stand' in the target language.
- The entire group then follows the instruction.
- Rapidly choose different children to come and roll the dice, say the command in the target language and then the whole group responds.
- Repeat until everybody has had a turn.

PLENARY

Ask the children to return to seat and use the command 'sit' in the target language. Throughout the lesson, use 'sit' or 'stand' in the target language and encourage the children to respond appropriately.

CONSOLIDATION ACTIVITIES

Other classroom commands could be taught in a similar way e.g. hands up, hands down, walk slow.

91. Big Art

Learning Objective

Securing

Pupils understand one or two simple classroom commands in the target language.

Additional Skills

Auditory: listening to target language.

Attention: focusing on an activity for 15 minutes (or more).

Fine motor: using pens.

Kinaesthetic: lying on tummy making large movements with arms.

Resources

Large white paper

Tape

Cushions for each child and adult

Selection of classical music on tablet/ computer and speakers

Red, green and yellow felt-tip pens for each person

MAIN

- Move the furniture out of the way and tape a very large piece of white paper on the floor, big enough so that each of the children can lie on their tummy around it.

- Place cushions at intervals so the children know how to position themselves. Next to each cushion, place a red, green and yellow felt-tip pen.

- Put some music on (classical but that changes pace) and invite the children to join the session.

- Adults model by lying down and getting a pen ready.

- Encourage everyone to start to draw along to the music.

- Lead adult to say a colour in the target language (either red, green or yellow) and see if the children understand the command. Adults model swapping colours.

- Change the music to create a different atmosphere and repeat changing the colours of the pens.

- Resist talking too much. Let the focus be the music and the target language.

PLENARY

Once the music selection has finished, encourage the children to put the lids on their pens. All sit up and look at their shared artwork.

CONSOLIDATION ACTIVITIES

Repeat this activity with different art materials or adding in more colours. The children could even take it in turns to say the colour in the target language.

131

92. Colour Race

Learning Objective

Securing

Pupils can respond briefly using single words, signs or symbols.

Additional Skills

Visual: recognising colour and matching it to an object.

Social communication: interacting with a partner to take part in the activity.

Auditory: processing and responding appropriately to a spoken instruction.

Resources

A range of objects in three colours familiar to the child in target language

Feely bag

Two sets of laminated large colour symbols matching the colours of the objects labelled in target language

MAIN

- To set up this activity, place all the coloured objects into the feely bag. Place the two sets of colour symbols side by side on a table top.

- Support each child to choose a classmate to join them in this lesson.

- Support the pair to come to the table and each sit behind a set of the colour symbols on the table top.

- Sit opposite the children, make a big show of pulling out a coloured object from the feely bag, hold up the object and ask 'What colour is the ....?' in the target language.

- The children then race to be the first to identify the colour, hold up the symbol and attempt to say the name of the colour in the target language.

- Repeat this until all the coloured objects in the feely bag have been shared.

PLENARY

Swap the roles around so that one of the children is asking the question and the adult and the other child are racing to respond. At the end of the session, count down '5, 4, 3, 2, 1, finished' in the target language and ask the children to return the objects to the feely bag using the target language.

CONSOLIDATION ACTIVITIES

This same lesson could be used with other words that might be being explored in the target language; for example, farm animals, numbers.

93. Old MacDonald

Learning Objective

Securing

Pupils may read and understand a few words presented in a familiar context with visual cues.

Additional Skills

Auditory: listening to and joining in with a familiar song.

Social communication: waiting for a turn as part of a group.

Visual: responding to visual cues at the appropriate time to contribute to the experience of the group.

Resources

Large written copy of the lyrics for 'Old MacDonald Had a Farm' in target language

Symbols of farm animals labelled in target language

Small world animal figures of farm animals

MAIN

- Support the children to come and sit in a semicircle ready to learn.

- Hold up/display the lyrics of 'Old MacDonald' in the target language and model singing the song in the target language, pointing at each word in turn.

- Encourage the whole group to sing the song in the target language.

- At the point in the song that describes which animal is on the farm, hold up an animal symbol and choose a child to identify the animal, ideally in the target language.

- Then support the child to find the correct small world animal figure to match the symbol and label it in the target language.

- The whole group then continues with the song.

- Repeat this until all the children in the group have had a turn identifying the animal on the farm from the written lyrics and/or the symbol in the target language.

PLENARY

Hold up an animal symbol and the child with that animal names it in the target language and gives it back to the adult to finish the session.

CONSOLIDATION ACTIVITIES

Look at other books with the child that tell stories about farm animals and use the animal symbols labelled in the target language to talk about them.

94. Numero Beetle

Learning Objective

Securing

Pupils may understand a few words in context with visual clues.

Additional Skills

Attention: focusing on an activity for 15 minutes (or more).

Fine motor: finding correct beetle piece and sticking it down.

Visual: matching number to target language word.

Social communication: playing a game with rules.

Resources

Blank paper

Glue stick

Beetle body, arms, legs, wings and antenna all cut out

Box

Dice

Access to a device to play a number song in target language

MAIN

- This game is based on the classic party game of 'Beetle'. Give each child in the group a blank sheet of paper and a glue stick.

- Place the body, the legs, the antenna and the wings for each beetle in a box in the centre of the group.

- Model saying the numbers 1 to 6 in the target language.

- There will be no winner, as the group will be building the beetle together.

- Stick the completed beetle with the numbers for each of the body parts on the board so that the children can see.

- One by one, ask a child to come and roll the dice and say the number in the target language; also show the dice number to the group if needed.

- Everyone then finds the piece of the beetle that matches the number and sticks this down.

- The strict rules are that you need the body first, but there can be flexibility with this.

- Continue to take turns until all the beetles have been made.

PLENARY

Play a number song in the target language to consolidate the numbers that the children have been hearing and using for the session.

CONSOLIDATION ACTIVITIES

Make some beetle sets and laminate the pieces; place these with a dice in a box so that the children can choose to play this together during either a maths or a language starter or plenary.

95. Shake Shake Shake!

Learning Objective

Securing

Pupils can copy out a few words with support.

Additional Skills

Tactile: experiencing mark making in various sensory media.

Attention: completing a task modelled by an adult as independently as possible.

Fine motor: mark making in sensory media.

Resources

A3 black paper

Flour

Sieves (one per child plus one for adult modelling)

Shallow trays (one per child)

Short, familiar words from target language printed and laminated

MAIN

- Support the children to come and sit in a semicircle ready to learn.

- Lay out the A3 black paper on the floor in front of the children.

- Pour some flour into the sieve and model 'shake, shake, shaking' the flour onto the black paper.

- Model choosing a short word in the target language (this could be supported by a symbol or prop), saying the word and then using the index finger to write the word in the flour. Repeat this process to model the activity again for the group.

- Give each child a tray with a sieve, a small amount of flour and a selection of short words in the target language.

- Each child takes the resources back to their place at the table and repeats the activity modelled by the adult as independently as possible.

PLENARY

Once the children have had time to practise their writing independently in the trays, call the group back to the semicircle. Then ask each child either to show a word they have written or to come to the front to write a word in the target language for the group.

CONSOLIDATION ACTIVITIES

Repeat this activity in other sensory media such as sand, cornflour, etc. Also gradually extend the length and variety of words in the target language that the children copy.

96. Fruit Tally

Learning Objective

Securing

Pupils can copy out a few words with support.

Additional Skills

Attention: focusing on an activity for 15 minutes (or more).

Fine motor: copying words.

Social communication: asking people questions.

Kinaesthetic: moving around to talk to people.

Resources

Visual with pictures of fruit and the names in target language

Blank tally sheet for each child

Pencils

Clipboards

MAIN

- Tell the children that today they are going to be finding out everyone's favourite fruit by doing a tally.

- Place the visual of the pictures of the fruit and the names in the target language on the table for each child along with a blank tally sheet and a pencil.

- Encourage the children to choose the 3–5 fruit they want to include in their tally and to copy the words to their tally sheet. Encourage them to draw a picture of the fruit to support remembering what the word says later in the session.

- Once everyone has finished, pack the visuals away. Give a clipboard to each child and help them to attach their tally sheet.

- Support (where needed) the children to ask their classmates, and potentially people outside of the class, what their favourite fruit is from the selection.

- The child makes a tally mark next to each response. (Make sure you have already taught tally marks; if not, practise this before the activity.)

PLENARY

Come back together and ask the children to count the tally marks for each fruit and give them a total. Ask them which fruit was the most popular.

CONSOLIDATION ACTIVITIES

You could use this information to plan a trip to the supermarket or greengrocer to buy fruit for snacks.

97. Classroom Calamity

Learning Objective

Securing

Pupils can label one or two objects.

Additional Skills

Social communication: working with a partner to complete a task.

Communication: using speech/symbols/sign to communicate meaning to a peer.

Kinaesthetic: moving in a controlled, calm way to complete a physical task.

Resources

Laminated symbols of common classroom objects labelled in target language e.g. chair, table, book, pencil

Blu Tack

MAIN

- When the whole class is ready to learn, show the children the classroom labels and the matching classroom objects and label them in the target language.

- Then divide the children into pairs and give them each a set of the laminated classroom labels.

- Ask the pairs to label these items in the classroom and name them in the target language e.g. sticking the chair symbol on a chair, the pencil symbol on the pencil pot.

- Congratulate the class for organising and labelling the classroom so well! Then send the children out to play or home for the day.

- Once all the children are out of the room, mix up all the labels so that e.g. the chair symbol is now on a book.

- When all the children are back in the classroom, explain there has been a terrible mix up! All the labels have been moved around and nothing is labelled correctly any more!

- Then ask the children to work in their pairs again to reorganise the labels so that they are correct.

PLENARY

After a short period allowing the children to reorganise the labels ask the children to stop and stand behind their chairs. Go around the classroom, hold up an object and ask what it is in the target language. Then check with the class that it has been labelled properly.

CONSOLIDATION ACTIVITIES

This process could be repeated in different areas of the school e.g. the soft play room, the PE hall.

98. Name That Animal

Learning Objective

Securing

Pupils can label one or two objects.

Additional Skills

Attention: focusing on an activity for 15 minutes (or more).

Fine motor: copying words.

Kinaesthetic: moving around to place labels.

Visual: matching pictures or words.

Resources

Large pictures of animals

Blu Tack

Labels for each child

Pencils

Visual with pictures of animals and the names in target language

Timer

MAIN

- Place large pictures of familiar animals around the room.

- At the tables, place a set of labels (a different colour for each child), pencils and a visual with pictures of the animals and the name in the target language.

- Spend time with the children copying out the words onto their set of labels. Encourage them to draw a picture so that they can remember to which animal the name matches.

- Once everyone has finished, tell the children that they have three minutes to label as many animal pictures as they can.

- Start the timer.

- Support if needed by pointing at the picture, rather than telling the child the answer directly.

- At the end of 3 minutes, stop the game.

PLENARY

Bring all the pictures back to the table, say the name of the animal in the target language and count how many labels each child was able to place. You can give the winner a prize if you want, but a well done and a clap are often enough to celebrate success.

CONSOLIDATION ACTIVITIES

Place the animal pictures around the room, encourage children to find pictures of the animals in books, on the Internet or in the small world toy tray and add to each of the 'displays'.

99. On a Picnic

Learning Objective

Securing

Pupils can, with some support, use the target language for a purpose.

Additional Skills

Communication: making a request to another person.

Social communication: taking part in a role play activity with a small group.

Tactile: tasting different foods.

Resources

Teddy bear per child

Picnic rug

Picnic food (ideally real)

Symbols of food labelled in target language (a set per child)

MAIN

- Support a small group of children to come on a teddy bears' picnic! Support each child to choose a bear and to come and sit on the picnic rug.

- Once everyone is seated, show the children each item of the picnic food, verbally label it in the target language and match it to the correct symbol.

- Then ask each child and teddy in turn what they want to eat.

- The child can use the symbol labelled in the target language or the target language word to request their preferred food for them and teddy to eat.

- Repeat this several times, each time encouraging the child to make the request using the target language.

PLENARY

Once the children are familiar with the food in the target language, support them to ask each other what they would like to eat, find the correct food and give it to their friends.

CONSOLIDATION ACTIVITIES

Using food symbols labelled in the target language the child could use the target language to request food at snack time or lunchtime (if they are a confident eater).

100. Fruit Shop

Learning Objective

Securing

Pupils use target language for a purpose.

Additional Skills

Attention: focusing on an activity for 15 minutes (or more).

Fine motor: handling money and peeling fruit.

Kinaesthetic: moving around to collect snack.

Visual: matching pictures or words.

Resources

Selection of real fruit

Till and real money

Price labels

Fruit names in target language

Red and white tablecloth

MAIN

- Set up a fruit shop role play in the class with real fruit, a till, the red and white tablecloth, money and price tickets. Label the fruit in the target language.

- An adult should be the shopkeeper the first time you play.

- As the children enter the room, give each of them some money. Tell them they have travelled to the country of their target language and they need to order the fruit that they want for a snack.

- All the children sit at the table and one at a time take a turn to enter the fruit shop. They can point at the fruit they would like, the adult will name it and the child will be encouraged to repeat the word in the target language.

- Once the child has chosen their preferred fruit, they pay with the money and return to the group to start eating. Another child then takes their turn.

PLENARY

Using the target language, name the fruit that everyone has chosen and encourage the children to join in.

CONSOLIDATION ACTIVITIES

Repeat this at snack time, perhaps once a week. Once the children are familiar with the names of the fruit in the target language and the process of requesting and serving, let them take a turn at being the shopkeeper.

101. Wacky Racing

Learning Objective

Securing

Pupils use target language for a purpose.

Additional Skills

Attention: focusing on an activity for 15 minutes (or more).

Fine motor: winding up the toys.

Kinaesthetic: moving to manipulate toys.

Visual: watching to see who has won.

Social communication: working as part of a group.

Resources

Masking tape

Box of windup toys

Whiteboard and pen

MAIN

- Place two strips of masking tape on the floor; one as the start line and one as the finish line, about 30cm apart.

- Place the box of windup toys at the start line; make sure that you have at least one for each child, but ideally a few more.

- Tell the children that it is race day and we need to find the fastest toy. On a whiteboard, write the names of each of the toys as the children choose the one they are going to race.

- Inform the children that the windup toys only understand instructions in the target language, and so they need to say, '1, 2, 3, go!' in the target language. Practise saying this together.

- Line all the children up along the start line; make sure this is long enough so everyone has space.

- Tell the children to wind up their toys and place them on the start line.

- All together, say, '1, 2, 3, go!' in the target language. Everyone should cheer on the toys.

- Once the winner is established, give them a point on the board, put all the toys back in the box and allow the children to choose again.

- Repeat.

PLENARY

Once everyone has had 3–5 turns, end the activity. Ask the children to put the toys back in the box. Check the board and ask the children to see if they can work out which toy won.

101. Wacky Racing *cont.*

CONSOLIDATION ACTIVITIES

Place the toys, the masking tape, whiteboard and pen all together in a box, and label it 'Wacky Racing'. The children can then have access to this as a choosing activity they can play together.

CPI Antony Rowe
Eastbourne, UK
October 30, 2023

- You may have found it hard to understand what other people might be thinking or feeling in a given situation. It is hard to interpret their facial expressions and body language to work out what they think or feel. If you can do this it helps to guide you about how you might best respond to them: what to do or what to say. Sometimes as the frontal cortex matures, it becomes easier to 'mind read' other people and see things from their point of view. This might be a good time to revisit some of the activities that you have done in social skills groups at school. It may all now begin to make more sense.

- As you get better at 'reading' other people and more skilful at choosing how to respond to them, working with other students in a group may become less stressful and more rewarding for you.

Of course, none of these changes will happen by magic. The maturing frontal cortex may just make it easier to change things in your life, if you work at what you want to change.

This book is written to support you through the process of starting at college and being successful during your time there and beyond.

Chapter 1

Making Choices

— — —

Making choices can be hard and stressful, but don't worry about it; it doesn't matter if you don't make the right one. The wrong one could be right later in life. You shouldn't worry about making choices. (student with autism in second year at further education college)

Next summer may seem a long time away and you will find it hard to think so far ahead, especially if you have exams before you leave school. But it is never too soon to start planning what you want to do when you leave school. This is one of the really big choices that we all have to face. Sometimes even making choices about everyday things like what to wear or which piece of homework to tackle first can be tricky. This chapter is to help you think about the choices for your future. The quizzes and activities included here can guide your decision making by leading you through some options.

In the UK, all young people are expected to stay in education or training until at least the age of 18. The most popular options for when you leave school are likely to be to:

- take A-levels in subjects that you enjoy and are good at

- choose vocational training at a college, if you already know the type of job you want to do

- take up an apprenticeship with an employer and attend college as a release student

- join a Foundation Stage course at college which will focus on learning and life skills.

Thinking about college

So, you are leaving school next summer and thinking about going to college. This is great if your teachers and family think it is a good idea, but why are YOU thinking of going to college? Record your reasons for going to college here.

■ COLLEGE OR NOT COLLEGE?

Reasons for going to college		Reasons for not going to college	
Do any of these apply to you? Tick any that you think are like you			
Treated more like an adult		Never been there before	
College is not like school		Lots of new people	
Get qualifications for a career		Not sure how to travel there	
I want to study (*favourite subject*) more		I want to earn money	
My friend(s) are going there		I learn best not studying	
What other reasons do you have for going to college or not going to college?			
Reasons for going to college		Reasons for not going to college	

What to do at college

You have decided that going to college is a good idea. The next thing to think about is what course to choose. It may help to think about what you enjoy doing. There may be some subjects at school that you would like to know more about but there may be other things that you enjoy such as gaming, gardening or sport. There are courses covering some of the activities that you have enjoyed doing out of school too. Record your activities that you enjoy the most here.

■ ENJOYMENT FACTORS

What I enjoy doing	
IN SCHOOL	**IN MY FREE TIME**

When you have put down your ideas, highlight the ones that you would like to do at college and that might help you to get a job later on.

A job after college

When you leave college, you will be looking for a job or planning to go on to higher education. It is not too soon to think about the sort of work that you would like. Record your ideas about aspects of work you may enjoy here.

◼ FACTORS OF WORKING

Work that suits me best would be...			
Do any of these apply to you? Tick any that you think suit you			
Work outdoors		Work indoors	
Work on my own		Work with other people	
Follow a regular routine		Do something different each day	
Work with animals		Work with computers	
Making or mending things		Find information from books or screens	
Having one base to work from		Move around bases	
Physically challenging work		Desk-based work	
Work with plants (horticulture)		Work with machines	
What ideas can you add to the list?			

You can also access these online tools to explore your strengths and match to some career suggestions.

- www.viacharacter.org/www/Character-Strengths-Survey

- www.teamtechnology.co.uk/careers/what-career-is-right-for-me.html

Qualifications

If you already have an idea about what you would like to do, what qualifications will you need? Look at the internet and ask people at school and at home.

■ QUALIFICATION CHECK

Qualifications I need

Job idea 1 is...

Qualifications needed...

Job idea 2 is...

Qualifications needed...

Job idea 3 is...

Qualifications needed...

Now be realistic, are they qualifications that you can achieve? If not, ask about other ways into that job, such as taking an apprenticeship. There are different levels of entry to many careers. For example, if you know the A-levels needed to get on a veterinary course are not likely to be achievable for you, colleges have veterinary nurse and animal care courses as alternative options.

Still no ideas? Have a look at these possibilities that will help you to think about what you would like to do.

■ MORE WORK IDEAS

No firm ideas yet?
Highlight any possibilities that interest you

Marketing	Selling	Financial services	
Art	Craft	Design	Photography
Cooking	IT	Gardening	Animals
Building	Mending	Machines	Carpentry
Engineering	Sport and leisure		Transport
Fire	Police	Security	Warehouse work
Children: nursery	Care work		Nursing
Medical technology	Paramedic		Doctor/dentist

Choosing a course

Now that you have some ideas about what you would like to do, get some prospectuses from your local colleges. You can find them online or your school will have copies for you to look at. Look at the courses on offer and any entry qualifications that are needed for them. Which course is the 'best fit' for you? You will be very lucky to find exactly what you had in mind, so think in terms of a 'best fit'. Do you have any back-up courses in mind that might suit you, if there are problems with your first choice?

■ MY TOP THREE COLLEGE COURSES

Course title	College	Qualifications needed	Length of course

Choosing a college

You have identified a preferred course and up to two back-up courses, so now it is time to think about the college itself. If you are thinking about colleges in two different local authorities, look at what is called their 'local offer', which you can find online. This will show you what support is available for students who have additional needs.

An example of the questions that may be answered within a 'local offer' can be seen here:

- What specific courses are available to students with learning difficulties and/or disabilities?

- How do I let the college know that I need extra help?

- How will the college support my learning?

- What specialist services and expertise are available at/or accessed by your education setting?

- Do staff supporting young people with learning needs and disabilities have training?

- How will I know that I am making progress?

- How will the college support my well-being?

- How will the college help me to transfer from school?

- How will the college support my progression and future employment?

- How accessible is the college environment?

- How can I be involved in my education setting?

- Who can I contact for further information?

Does your first choice of college have an open day or evening for students who are thinking about joining the college? The college website will show this, or teachers at school will know about the arrangements. Your school might take groups of students to visit the local colleges. Going with your friends and a teacher who knows the college will give you opportunities to ask questions.

If your school does not arrange a visit or a taster day to the college you have chosen, find out from their website when they have an open day or evening and ask your teacher or parents to arrange a visit and go with you.

Visiting a college

To make the best use of your visit to a college, it is helpful to have a checklist of things to find out. Your visit will help you to think about how you would get to the college each day from your home. When you visit, you will usually be given a map of the campus with the teaching rooms and other key areas on it. How easy will it be to find your way around?

When you visit, you will also meet a member of the college staff who can answer your questions, such as where you can go if you do not have any lessons.

The checklist below has some questions to guide your first impressions of the college.

■ FIRST IMPRESSIONS

Use this checklist and make notes during and after your visit.

1. How easy is it to get to college?

2. How easy is it to find my way around the campus?

3. Are the specialist rooms, laboratories and workshops well equipped?

4. Where do students go if they do not have a lesson?

5. Is there a base or lockers where I can store my equipment?

6. What are the canteen and lunch arrangements?

7. What are the students wearing?

8. What support is available for learning or if I feel anxious?

9. What clubs or sporting activities are offered?

10. Are the students and staff easy to talk to (i.e. friendly)?

Which college?

You have visited some colleges and looked at their courses and what they can offer you.

Does one stand out clearly as best for you? If not, you may have to make a decision about whether going to a place where you feel most comfortable is more or less important than getting the course you like the most. You may know someone who goes to the college. If you do, ask them about the college to help you to decide.

They will be able to talk about the college from the point of view of a student. Use this worksheet to help you decide.

■ WHICH COLLEGE IS BEST FOR ME?

	College A	College B
In favour: positive factors		
Against: negative factors		

Chapter 2

Preparation for Change

— ·· — ·· —

I had to do work experience. It helped me build my confidence. I felt like an adult. (student with autism in second year at further education college)

You have chosen the college that is right for you. Now you have some time to get to know more about the college and how it will be different from school, to help you to be ready for your first day.

Your school may arrange for someone from the college to visit you at your school so they can talk to you and your teachers about what has helped you to learn and feel comfortable in school. This may be a good opportunity to ask questions about the college and the support that it will be able to offer you.

Ask the special educational needs co-ordinator (SENCO) at your school if they can arrange a visit to the college that you have chosen so that you can explore the environment and meet the key people who will be working with you. If several of your classmates are going to the same college, the SENCO will probably arrange for a group of you to visit at the same time. It would be really helpful if you could meet your tutor and some of your teachers, but the college may not be able to allocate students to particular classes much before the start of the new term.

Your key worker

Most colleges will introduce you to your key worker who will ask you about your strengths, any difficulties that you have and the sort of learning support that you have found helpful in the past.

Some students like to have a support assistant available in classes who will engage with you when you ask for help but leave you to get on independently the rest of the time. Other students prefer to go to the learning support department when they need help.

Be confident to explain to your key worker any specific anxieties that you have about learning or socializing with the other students. They will be the person who can talk to other staff or make special arrangements to make you feel more comfortable at college.

Your key worker will be the person to keep in touch by email during the summer. They will email your timetable, as soon as it becomes available, so that you can familiarize yourself with it before you start. They will also let you know the arrangements for your first day, so that you know where to go and who will meet you.

Peer mentor

Some colleges will have a peer mentor scheme. A peer mentor is someone who is already attending college and has similar needs to you. They will have experience of managing their learning needs and social relationships at college. Talking to someone who may have had similar anxieties about starting at college can be very reassuring. Your peer mentor may also be one of the first people to talk to if you have any problems when you start college.

Know yourself

You have been at school for many years and will have a good idea about how you respond in the classroom.

Use the following tool to map your learning experience.

Share your learning map with your mentor and discuss what arrangements can be put in place to address the difficulties.

■ MAPPING YOUR LEARNING EXPERIENCE

The learning environment
Subject preferences

You may be studying different subjects in college and some we find easier and more interesting than others. Rate the subjects on the list on a scale of 1–5.

1	2	3	4	5
I avoid this subject	I do not like this subject	I tolerate this subject	I like this subject	I really enjoy this subject

For example, if you really enjoy maths...

List of subjects	Rating
Maths	5

My subject ratings are...

Subject	Rating

Classes involve different ways of working and some we will find more comfortable than others. Use the 5-point rating scale to indicate how you feel about different things that happen in classes.

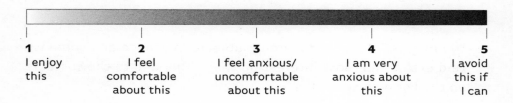

1	**2**	**3**	**4**	**5**
I enjoy this	I feel comfortable about this	I feel anxious/ uncomfortable about this	I am very anxious about this	I avoid this if I can

	1	2	3	4	5
1 Answering questions in class					
2 Listening when the teacher explains what we are going to do in the lesson					
3 Following instructions					
4 Knowing what to do to start a task					
5 Working on my own					
6 Working with a learning partner					
7 Working in a group					
8a Asking a teacher for help when I have not understood something					
8b Asking a fellow student for help when I have not understood something					
9 Working in a quiet class					

10 Working when other students are messing about	1 2 3 4 5
11 Reading aloud in class	1 2 3 4 5
12 Written work – handwriting	1 2 3 4 5
13 Recording what I have done using pictures, diagrams or graphs	1 2 3 4 5
14 Using the computer to record what I have done	1 2 3 4 5
15 When I go into class and my usual teacher is not there, but a cover	1 2 3 4 5
16 When our class has been moved to a different room	1 2 3 4 5
17 Making sure that I have all the books and equipment I need for the class	1 2 3 4 5
18 Writing down assignments so that I can understand what to do when I get home	1 2 3 4 5
19 When I have a support adult supporting me in class	1 2 3 4 5
20 When I have to stop what I am doing before I have finished	1 2 3 4 5
21 When the teacher writes down what we have to do as well as telling us	1 2 3 4 5

22 When the teacher uses pictures, diagrams, videos, etc. to help to explain things	1	2	3	4	5
23 Homework assignments	1	2	3	4	5
24 Sharing equipment in practical lessons	1	2	3	4	5
25 When other students try to distract me	1	2	3	4	5
26 When the teacher introduces a new topic I know little or nothing about	1	2	3	4	5
27 Class tests and assessments	1	2	3	4	5

Look at your rating about what happens in class. Describe your ideal class/lesson.

What I need to know

There will be many questions about college that you need to know the answers to in order to feel comfortable.

Next are some questions that you may want to ask when you visit your college. There are some examples but you will need to add your own ideas. Remember to take your list with you when you visit.

■ QUESTIONS FOR COLLEGE STAFF

1. How will you let me know in advance if there are any changes of teacher or room?

2. Will there be someone in class to help me with my work?

3. Will I have time in the learning support base (or similar) to help with work or homework?

4. If the classroom is noisy and I cannot concentrate, what do I do? Where can I go?

5. What will happen if I get lost and am late for a class?

6. Is there a quiet place for me to go when there are no lessons or to eat lunch?

7. What will happen if I lose things?

8. Who can I talk to if I feel angry or upset?

These are just some examples of questions that students ask. What are your questions?

Timetables

Ask your key worker if you can look at an example of a timetable for your course. You may find it rather different from the sort of timetable you are used to. There may be times when there are no classes to go to or days when the students go on work experience. Discuss with your key worker what students do when they do not have classes.

■ EXAMPLE TIMETABLE WITH 'FALLOW' PERIODS

Monday		History	ICT	
Tuesday			Maths	Maths
Wednesday		ICT	Sports club	
Thursday		Maths	History	History
Friday		Sports club		

Grey periods are 'fallow' times – which are free study times.

For some courses, there will be days when you go out on work experience. Talk to your key worker about the arrangements that are made about this, if your course includes work experience.

■ SAMPLE TIMETABLE WITH WORK EXPERIENCE

Monday		Functional skills		
Tuesday			Work experience	Work experience
Wednesday		Work experience	Work experience	
Thursday		Functional skills		
Friday		Sports club		

Grey periods are 'fallow' times – which are free study times.

Your key worker will send you a copy of your real timetable as soon as it is finalized. Look at it carefully:

- What time is your first class each day? Is it the same time each day?

- What time does your last class finish? Is it the same time each day?

- Will you have to think about when you need to be in college each day and what that will mean for getting there?

- Look at the classrooms, laboratories and workshops on your timetable. Check on your map that you can find them.

- Does your timetable show times when you can go to the learning support department?

- Check the length of the lessons. They may be longer than you are used to.

- Will it be hard for you to stay in a class for that long without a learning break? If so, discuss this with your mentor.

Navigation

You will have been given a map of your college campus on your visit before you left school. Don't worry if you have lost it, as there will be one on the college website. It may seem a long time ago that you made your visit and it will all seem more real now you have your timetable. Many colleges will have an induction day for new students. This will give you the opportunity to explore the college with your map and your actual timetable. You may be with a group of new students and you can explore together. It may be a good idea to exchange email addresses with anyone you get on well with. All colleges will have different buildings to navigate.

Using the map of your college, make sure that you can get:

- from your entrance to the lockers and cloakrooms

- from your cloakroom/entrance to all the classrooms on your timetable

- from each of your classrooms to the others, to the canteen, library, any laboratories or workshops and the nearest toilets.

There may be some spaces like the crowded entrance hall that you might like to avoid at busy times. Are there any alternative ways of getting to where you need to go?

Walk the walk. There is no substitute for walking round a building and taking notes of markers such as 'The stairs to room 6 are just after that poster on the wall'. It may be possible to take a photograph to help you remember, but you will need to ask permission from college staff before you do this. Once the space is crowded with people it will be more difficult to spot where the stairs are or where corridors meet. Try to take as much time as you need to feel comfortable that you can find your way around.

When you have explored the campus, you may feel that there are some areas that feel less comfortable than others. Use the map of your college to map 'My Landscape' of the college. When you have become more familiar with the environment, you may decide to change some of your first impression codings.

■ MAPPING THE ENVIRONMENTAL LANDSCAPE

The physical environment

- Look carefully at the map of your college.

- Use the highlighter pens to mark how the areas on the map make you feel.

Green = I feel calm and relaxed in this space

Yellow = I feel anxious/uncomfortable in this space

Red = I would like to avoid this space as it makes me very anxious

- For the areas that you have coloured red, are there any circumstances, for example time of day, which make you feel safer?

- What might the college staff do to help you feel safer in your 'red' areas?

Sensory issues

As you go around college, you may feel uncomfortable in some areas where the lighting is glaring or the noise levels are high. If you visit on a day when the students are all there, you may find crowded stairways or corridors or a busy, noisy canteen area that you would like to avoid. You may already be aware that your senses are more sensitive than those of most people. We have five senses that give us information about our surroundings. They are sight, hearing, smell, taste and touch. You probably know which of those senses causes you problems:

- Can't concentrate when the strip lights flicker?

- Loud noises make you want to leave the room?

- Hate going into the canteen because of the smell?

- Stick to the same mild foods?

- Dislike being touched by or being too close to people?

We have two other senses that are less obvious:

- *Proprioception:* This sense tells us where our bodies are in space. Try an experiment. Shut your eyes, hold out your arm, turn it palm up and palm down. The messages to your brain tell you which way up your hand is without you having to look. Some people need to 'fidget' in order to keep checking where their body is in space.

- *Balance:* The balance system is, unexpectedly, found in your inner ear. When you try to stand on one leg or climb the stairs your balance system is sending messages to your brain. Some people need to hold on to a rail when they go down stairs in order to feel safe.

Use this checklist to explore your sensory sensitivities.

■ SENSORY SENSITIVITY CHECKLIST

Is this like you? Tick the boxes			
	YES	NO	Don't know
I like to keep things the same: routines are important to me. I dislike change			
It is hard to recognize people I know in unfamiliar places or wearing different clothes			
I dislike bright lights			
I am easily distracted by patterns, e.g. stripes on carpets or curtains			
I am good at remembering how to get to places			
I am scared of lifts and heights			
I avoid catching/throwing ball games			
I am uncomfortable in crowded noisy places			
I am uncomfortable about being touched, including shaking hands			
I found it hard to learn to ride a bike			
I put my hands over my eyes or turn away from bright lights			
Crowded stairways worry me			
I find it easier to listen when not looking at a person			
I get lost easily			
I know a lot about my favourite topics			
I prefer to sit at the front, back or side of a group			

I am upset by some sounds			
I can hear sounds that others can't hear			
I dislike the feel of some fabrics or substances			
I don't always notice when I am hurt			
I dislike the texture or smell of some foods			
I really enjoy some activities like trampolining, swings and adventure park rides			
I like a hug but only if I ask for it (initiate it)			
I have to be reminded to wear a coat on a cold day and take my jumper off on a hot day			
I like the feel of some materials			
I am upset by smells that others seem to ignore			
I often bump into people or objects			
I like to stick to the same foods rather than try something new			
I struggle with fastenings and handwriting			
I feel anxious or worried a lot of the time			

Share your answers with your key worker or mentor. Talk about the things you are sensitive to or find hard.

(Adapted from the Inclusion Development Programme's adult sensory profile checklist)

Sensory overload

If you are in a setting where one or more of your senses are getting too much information at once, it can be very uncomfortable. A crowded shop with bright lights and loud music may need a quick exit. We all try to keep our senses at a comfortable level, which we call our comfort zone. If we are getting too much or too little stimulation from our senses we will try to get back to that comfort zone.

This is how it works.

■ THE COMFORT ZONE

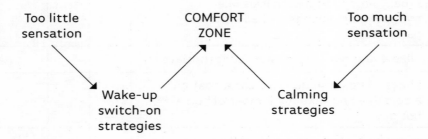

Mostly, we need to try to calm down. Here are some things that people do to get back to their comfort zone.

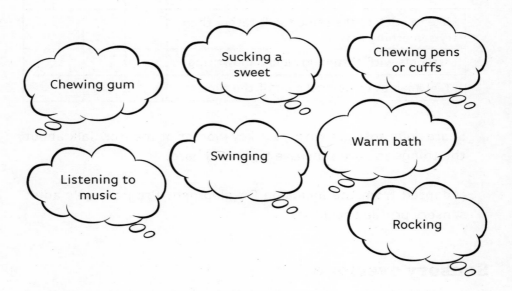

Here are some empty bubbles for your own ideas.

Sometimes we may need to feel more alert/switched on. Here are some things that people do.

Here are some empty bubbles for your own ideas.

Look at what is in the bubbles. Which ones would work in a classroom? We will talk again about keeping calm in Chapter 8.

Chapter 3

Early Days

— ◆ — ◆ — ◆ —

I was nervous when I first started; all the classes were different to my old college. (student with autism in second year at further education college)

Starting anything new is always a bit daunting. The first days at college will feel more under control if you are really well organized. This chapter is about being prepared for that first day.

Getting to college

Not many people are lucky enough to live so close to their college that they can walk. You may have had a taxi or mini-bus to take you to your old school, but this is not usually an option when you attend college. You may be eligible for transport but this will depend on the policy of your local authority. Look it up online or ask your SENCO at school to advise you.

If you do not live in a town, there may be a college bus that picks people up from the local villages. If this is you, find out where the nearest pick-up point is and the time that the bus leaves. The college website will help you with this sort of information. Most students will either get a lift from family or friends or use public transport: a bus or a train.

Getting a lift

If you are hoping for a lift, look at your timetable with the driver. On some days, you may start and finish at different times. Can you still get a lift if you have a 10am start rather than the usual 8.30am?

Some scenarios to consider:

- My lift can only get me to college for 9am at the latest. On Thursday I have a 10.30am start. Do I go in for 9am and then wait around? Is there somewhere I can go to catch up on my work? Do I catch a bus or train on that day?

- My classes finish at 3pm on a Wednesday. My lift can't pick me up before 4.30. Do I stay in college? Is there a homework club to go to? Is there a leisure/sports club to go to? Do I catch a bus or train home on that day?

If your timetable includes work experience, you will need to talk to the driver about the different arrangements for those days.

Public transport

Most students will be using public transport. The summer break is a good time to practise catching a bus or a train. Here are some things to find out in advance:

- Are you eligible for a bus or train pass at a reduced student rate? (Look online.)

- Where is the nearest bus/train stop to your house?

- Can you walk there?

- What time does the bus/train leave that will get you to college on time? The time may be different on some days.

Use this worksheet to work out your timings.

■ BUS OR TRAIN TIMES

Day	Start of college	Bus/train time	End of college	Bus/train time
Monday				
Tuesday				
Wednesday				
Thursday				
Friday				

If you are going by bus and do not have a student pass, find out the cost of the fare. It is helpful if you have the correct change to give to the driver.

If you are going by train, there may be a ticket machine. Practise using it before your first day. There may be a ticket office. Practise asking for a ticket to get to where you need to go. Take time over the summer to practise that journey until you feel comfortable about how long it takes and the clues that tell you where to get off. You may like someone to go with you at first, but aim to be confident to do it on your own before your first day.

Just in case the bus or train is late, or you miss it, put an app on your iPhone with the college number so that you can explain why you will be late. Keep the time of the next bus or train on your iPhone too.

Getting the timings right

The bus or train and even, maybe, your lift will not wait for you if you are late. What time will you need to get up each day to get to college on time?

Use the worksheet below to time your morning routine.

■ MORNING ROUTINE

How long does it take?	Time yourself
ACTIVITY	**MINUTES**
Wash/shower	
Find clothes	
Get dressed	
Hair/makeup	

Breakfast	
Bag check	
Anything else?	
TOTAL TIME	

How long do you take to get ready to leave the house? Now add on the time it will take to get to your bus or train. What time does your bus or train leave? Work back from that time to calculate when you will need to set your alarm clock.

Use the worksheet below to help you with the calculation. You may have different timings for some days. Use this plan to calculate for each day. You may want to build in a little extra time each day so that you do not feel rushed, or under pressure.

■ TIMINGS TO GET UP

1. Morning routine	Takes _____ minutes
Leave the house at	_____ am
2. Walk to bus/train	Takes _____ minutes
3. Time of bus/train	_____ am

3 – 2 – 1 = time to set the alarm clock.

An example of using the plan: On Monday, I have to be at the bus stop at 8.10am so I can be in college by 8.45. My morning routine takes me 45 minutes, without having to rush. It takes me 10 minutes to walk to the bus stop. I will need to be up by 7.15 on Mondays. On some days it will be different.

The night before

It will save you time in the mornings if you get things ready the night before. Your 'to do' list could be:

- Look at your timetable for the next day.

- Is there any work to hand in?

- Is your basic equipment in your bag?

- Is there any specific equipment needed for that day (e.g. sports kit)?

- Do you have your money for fares or your student pass?

- Do you have money for lunch or is your packed lunch ready in the fridge? (You might use a post-it note to remind you to collect it in the morning.)

- Do you have your mobile? (Remember to switch it off in class.)

Use this checklist as a prompt.

■ THE NIGHT BEFORE...

Check:	
Basic equipment	
Money for lunch	
Money for fares	
Phone	
Homework due	

Any extra equipment for:	
Monday	
Tuesday	
Wednesday	
Thursday	
Friday	

It may be helpful to check the weather for the next day so you can have the clothes you plan to wear ready for the morning.

Some students find it helpful to have a large zip-up wallet with a different colour of zip for each subject. The equipment that is needed for that subject is always kept in the wallet: basic equipment such as pens and paper but also what is specific for that subject such as a ruler, projector and compass for maths. If work needs to be handed in for a lesson, it can be put in the wallet for that subject. This strategy makes it easier to ensure that you have everything you need for a lesson and can get things out of your bag quickly at the start of a lesson.

Remembering to hand in work on the right day can be tricky. Some students have found the stacker tray system helpful. Work to be done is put in the stack on the left in the tray marked with the day you need to do the work. Finished work is put in the right-hand stack in the tray marked for the day the work is needed to be handed in.

■ THE STACKER BOX SYSTEM

To do		Hand in
Monday		Monday
Tuesday		Tuesday
Wednesday	**DESK**	Wednesday
Thursday		Thursday
Friday		Friday
Weekend		

Case study: Charlie

Charlie was introduced to the stacker box system at school, but despite encouragement from his mother he never really used it. When Charlie went to college, he surprised his mother by asking if they could set up the stacker boxes again to help him to organize his work. He could now see the use of the system for himself and took responsibility for using it.

Day one

You have got to college on time and with everything you need. Phew, well done.

Go to the place where you have arranged to meet your mentor/ key worker. Don't panic if they are not there yet – they may have been held up for some reason. Do something to keep calm while you wait, like reading the wall posters. When they arrive, try to look at them, smile and say 'hello'. You should already know what to expect next.

Meeting your group

Remember, it is everyone's first day and they will be feeling anxious too, even if they don't show it. Try to 'walk tall' and go into the room looking confident. Is there someone that you recognize from your old school or from one of your college visits? You may even have been in contact with them during the summer by email. Do you remember practising how to open a conversation when you were at school? Now is the time to put some of this into practice. Good conversation openers may be:

'Alright? Are you a bit nervous too?'
'Hi, is it your first day as well?'
'Hi, I am (*name*).'
'I think we are in the right place.'

At the end of your first day, take some time to reflect on what went well for you.

Use the worksheet below to record your reflections. Share your positive thoughts with your family.

■ WHAT WENT WELL TODAY?

1	
2	
3	
4	
5	

What would I change?

There may still be some nagging worries about starting at your new college. Some students have found it helpful to record these.

Use the 'Start of college questionnaire' to clarify your thoughts. If you give any of the statements a rating of between 7 and 10, share those concerns with your mentor or key worker.

■ START OF COLLEGE QUESTIONNAIRE

Rate each of the statements between 1 and 10 depending on how worried or anxious you are about them, with 1 being not worried at all and 10 being the most worried you have ever felt.

Are you anxious or worried about...	Rating
Getting to and from college (transport arrangements)	
Being bullied or teased at college	
Making friends at college	
Controlling your temper or frustration at college when things don't go right	
Unexpected changes to your timetable, teachers or classroom	
Where you are going to sit in the classroom	
Who is going to sit next to you in the class	
Entering your classroom on the first day	
Meeting your teacher	
Having a learning support assistant to support you in class	
Getting to class on time	
Not being able to keep up with note taking in class	

Finding the work too difficult	
Finding coursework difficult	
Being organized so you have the right notes and books for the right class	
Being organized so you get your coursework and homework done on time	
Exam arrangements: getting a separate room, extra time, etc.	
Sudden noises in class, e.g. fire alarm, 'explosive' experiment	
Noisy classrooms in general	
Specific noises such as an electric motor sound	
Specific smells, e.g. chemicals or perfume	
Being asked to work with another student in the class or in a group	
Being asked by the teacher to answer a question in class	
Being asked by the teacher to read aloud in class	
Doing a presentation in front of the class	
Doing experiments in physics or chemistry	
Asking for help from the teacher when you don't understand something	
Where you are going to eat your lunch	
Where you are going to spend break times	
Where you are going to study during your free periods	
Where you can go if you want to get away from everyone and have some quiet time	
Who to go and see if you have a worry or problem at college	

Chapter 4

In the Classroom

I was nervous when I first went into the classrooms at college because they were different to my classrooms at school. (student with autism in first year at apprenticeship college)

Getting to class

Remember that you chose to come to college to learn new things, so it is important to go to your lessons. If there is something about a class that makes you feel anxious, discuss this with your mentor. There is usually a way of solving the problem to make you feel more comfortable.

You will have visited the classroom before the start of term and may have met your teachers and support assistants or at least know their names and have a photograph of them on your email. Although lining up is not a regular aspect of college life, you may sometimes have to wait for a teacher to come to unlock a room such as a science lab. If you find waiting with a crowd of people hard, try standing back and looking busy: check your bag, your phone, your notes or look at a book. When the teacher comes, you can file in with the others.

Mostly the students will go straight into the room and find a seat. This can be quite stressful for anyone, although few will admit it. The anxiety is usually social: will X choose to sit with me or will she go with Y? Then what will I do? It is much easier for everyone if the teacher allocates seats for the students so you know exactly where to go.

You may have particular sensitivity about where you sit:

- Away from a window as the light or noise is distracting.

- Away from noisy heating pipes.

- At the back or side of the room so you do not feel crowded and vulnerable and are less overlooked by other students.

- At the front of the room so you can concentrate better on what the teacher is saying.

- Away from distracting wall charts.

Record your own preferences on the worksheet. If possible, discuss these with your mentor and teachers before you join the class.

■ SEATING PREFERENCES

My preferred seating is...
This is because...

Changes

Sometimes you may have to go to a different room for your class. Often the staff will know in advance and tell you, for example, that the next class will be in the laboratory to do practical work. Your teacher may know that they will not be taking the next lesson because they are, for example, going on a training course. They will usually be able to tell you who will be taking the class instead of them. Your mentor can remind you of the cover teacher's name and even show you a photo of them. Any planned changes will be sent to your email in advance.

You can prepare for planned changes, so they are less likely to make you feel anxious. However, some changes happen, due to illness or accidents, that cannot be foreseen. You may not get advance warning of these until you arrive at college. If you feel you can face the uncertainty of finding a new room or meeting a new teacher, then fine. If not, it may be time to find your mentor for some support.

Listening to instructions

A lesson will usually start with the teacher reviewing the last lesson, introducing a new topic and giving some instructions. This will involve a lot of careful listening. Most teachers will know that it is easier to understand new ideas if they use visual support such as maps, diagrams or demonstrations to supplement the actual words they use. This is particularly important if they are introducing new terms such as, for example, 'pixelated' in art or 'plate tectonics' in geography. You may find the first part of the lesson difficult.

- You may find it hard to listen and concentrate for a long time without a 'listening break' so you lose track of what the teacher is saying.

- You may need a little more time to follow what the teacher is saying as the information is coming too quickly for you to process it.

- You may be concentrating on a piece of work and not realize that the teacher has started talking to the class and you have missed the crucial first part of what was said.

If you experience any of these things, don't sit and panic, get some help. You may already have some ideas about what is helpful for you.

Use the worksheet below to record what helps you to listen and understand.

■ WHAT HELPS YOU LISTEN AND UNDERSTAND?

What helps me to listen and understand...
This is because...

If there are still some problems, do you feel confident to tell your teachers that you don't understand? Sometimes when we are anxious we do not always choose our words carefully. Shouting out 'I can't do this' may not be the best idea. You might try one of the following:

- Practise a form of words that sounds polite: 'I am not sure how to do this, please will you help me?' Remember to put up your hand.

- If you don't like to ask for help in front of the other students, go up to the teacher when they have finished talking to the group.

- It may help to have a card that you put on the desk or hold up, so the teacher knows that you need help.

- If you have support in class, your support assistant may write some notes while the teacher is talking and go through them with you until you are confident that you understand.

- If there are written notes or handouts for the topic, go through these highlighting the main ideas.

- You may be allowed to record your lessons so that you can go through what is said later and at your own pace.

When asked, most teachers will say that they do not expect students to take notes in lessons, but the students say that this is expected as a matter of routine. This may present particular difficulty if your handwriting is slow or you find it hard to summarize the main ideas as you go along. Usually arrangements can be made for you to record what is said, have handouts to highlight or have a support assistant to take notes for you.

Your preferred strategy may not be any of the ones that worked for other students. You are unique.

Record your preferred strategies on the worksheet here.

■ PREFERRED STRATEGIES

My preferred strategies are...

This is because...

Learning channel preferences

We all use many styles of learning. How we choose to learn often depends on the type of task. There was a popular idea some years ago that we all have a preferred learning style.

The learning channel preferences questionnaire may give you some ideas about how you learn. You will probably identify strategies from each category, but you may find one of them is stronger for you.

LEARNING CHANNEL PREFERENCE QUESTIONNAIRE

For each statement decide which applies to you.

Almost always: Score 5
Often: Score 4
Sometimes: Score 3
Rarely: Score 2
Almost never: Score 1

	Score
Visual	
I remember something better if I write it down.	
I can visualize pictures in my head.	
It is easy for me to understand maps, charts, diagrams.	
If I am trying to remember something new, like a new word, it helps me to make a picture in my head.	
It is easier for me to work in a quiet place.	
Auditory	
I need to discuss things to understand them better.	
I prefer it if someone tells me how to do things rather than having to read instructions.	
I remember what people say better than what they look like.	
I prefer to record my work rather than write or type it.	
When reading, I listen to the words in my head or read aloud.	
Kinaesthetic	
I would rather start doing or be shown what to do than listen to or read instructions.	
I need frequent breaks when studying.	
I think better if I can move around.	
I dislike proofreading my work.	
I would rather do a practical project than write a report.	

Add up your scores for each section and work out which section you get most points for.

Visual: Ideas to try if you are mostly a visual learner

If the results from the questionnaire show you are predominantly a visual learner, you might try some of the following strategies.

Imaging

The construction of images is a very personal experience. The pictures inside your head are yours alone. An example of imaging: You are trying to remember the sequence of plants on a mountain. Imagine walking up the mountain. The valley floor is flat and the ground feels boggy, you can see rushes. As you leave the valley floor, you feel the grass damp on your legs. Climbing up through the trees, what trees can you name? Then the heather moor, how does that feel on your legs? Walk the climb in your mind to recall the sequence of the vegetation. You might find imaging helps you remember how to pronounce new words like tsunami (a big, usually destructive wave).

There is also a technique called cued spelling, which uses imaging to support spelling. Ask your key worker to show you how this works.

Icons and symbols

These can be memorable and help you with note taking in class. For example:

^ = the
& = and

Icons can represent objects, for example == for a Bunsen burner, and concepts such as a globe for 'universal'.

Procedural flow charts

These are to show what you need to do in order to complete a task such as taking a soil sample. The task is broken down into small steps – this is called task analysis. You may need some help to do this at first, but with practice you will learn to do it yourself. The flow chart tells you what to do and the order to do it.

Look below for a simple example.

■ A PROCEDURAL FLOWCHART – TO MAKE A CUP OF TEA

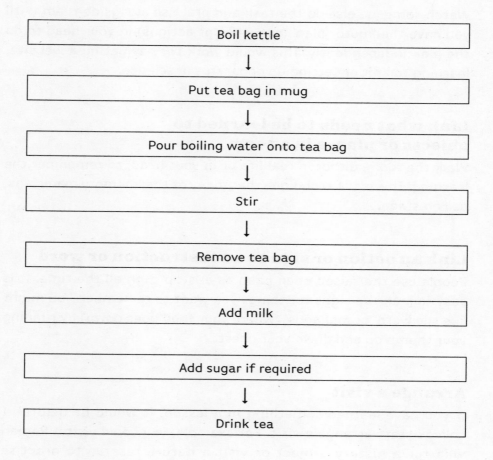

Boil kettle

↓

Put tea bag in mug

↓

Pour boiling water onto tea bag

↓

Stir

↓

Remove tea bag

↓

Add milk

↓

Add sugar if required

↓

Drink tea

Remember that your timetable, diary and calendar are all visual prompts that everyone uses every day. How often do you see people making lists?

Kinaesthetic: Ideas to try if you're mostly a kinaesthetic learner

If the results from the questionnaire show you are predominantly a kinaesthetic learner, you might try some of the following strategies.

Learn by doing

Watch someone else do the task and practise alongside them until you have the 'motor plan' (sequence of actions) in your head to do the plan independently. This would work for navigating a website, learning to knit or setting up apparatus in science.

Link what needs to be learned to objects or places in a room

Walk the room, either in real life or in your head, to remember the learning. This is the technique that many of the 'memory magicians' use on stage.

Link an action or sign to an instruction or word

People use the raised open palm as a 'stop' sign all the time. It is easy to make up signs for things you want to remember. You might cue the word 'oesophagus' (where your food goes down) by running your thumb up and down your chest.

Arrange a visit

If you have learned something in a lesson, it would be helpful if college staff arrange a visit. For example, you could visit a Roman villa for a history project or visit a nature reserve to practise identifying types of tree or fungi.

Auditory: Ideas to try if you're mostly an auditory learner

If the results from the questionnaire show you are predominantly an auditory learner, you might try some of the following strategies.

Repeating aloud

Keep repeating aloud to yourself what you want to remember. This is called rehearsal and it helps you put information in your long-term memory.

Silly rhymes and sentences

Make up silly rhymes and sentences to match the learning and help you remember. For example, for bones in the arm: huge, ugly rats catch men playing – huge (humerus), ugly (ulna), rats (radius), catch (carpals), men (metacarpals), playing (phalanges). Can you recall the colours of the rainbow? Richard of York gave battle in vain.

Link new to existing information

Link new information to what you already know; for example, they grow coffee in Kenya, so link it to the work you have already done on coffee growing in Brazil.

Group work

You will be expected to complete some tasks independently but at other times you will be asked to work with a partner or as a member of a group. 'Get into groups of four' may be the most dreaded instruction that a teacher can give, if you are expected to organize this for yourself. Working alone may not be an option if the task needs several people to complete it successfully.

At work, you may not have a choice about working on your own, so this should be a last resort at college. It is important to practise the skills of working with other people.

Your teacher should know if you find group work a challenge and make arrangements to help, such as:

- letting you work with a support assistant

- allocating you to a carefully selected group of students that you feel comfortable to work with

- asking a support assistant to work with your group to mediate on your behalf, if necessary

- allocating you a task in your group that matches your strengths. For example, if you like to be accurate, you might do the measurements for an experiment; if you are good at maths, you could calculate scores; if you are good on the computer, you could enter results on a spreadsheet.

Joining in and successfully participating in a group requires quite complex social skills. You probably practised some of them at school. If you listen to what others are saying it is easier to time your participation, i.e. when to speak. Think about whether it is the right moment to ask a question or to give your views.

If you are passionate about a topic, it may be easy to get carried away and dominate the discussion. Other people will usually not appreciate this. If you are not particularly interested in the topic, you may feel like withdrawing from the discussion altogether and others may think this is discourteous. Sometimes it is hard to listen to what others say, especially if you disagree with them or think they are talking rubbish. Try to put your point of view forward calmly and politely. Everyone is entitled to an opinion! We will talk more about developing successful communication skills in Chapter 6.

Often there is not just one way to carry out a task or solve a problem. You might have an idea about the way you think is right and would work best, but other people in the group may not agree with you and think that a different way is better. It is sometimes hard not to get angry or upset if your solution is not favoured by others. Group members tend to favour the ideas offered by the most popular or assertive member of the group even if it is not the best solution.

This is one of the downsides of placing more emphasis on relationships rather than facts and logic.

Think about the best strategy if the discussion is not going your way.

Good ideas	Bad ideas
• Writing down your solution (this will help you to keep calm) • Try their idea first, then suggest yours • If you are placed in a group that is difficult for you, do tell your teacher or mentor	• Shouting about how good your idea is and how the alternative is wrong or won't work • Storming off, leaving the group

Use the worksheet below to record your strategies for group work. Share your ideas with your mentor and teacher.

▪ STRATEGIES FOR GROUP WORK

My strategy for group work is...

I will try to negotiate by...

Practical work

The courses that you have chosen may involve practical work in a workshop or laboratory. In these settings there are often machines, tools or chemicals that are potentially dangerous and need to be handled with care. Your teacher or lab technician will explain the safety rules for that setting. If you are sensitive to certain materials or fastenings and you have to wear protective clothing, ask to try it on in advance. If there is a problem, the staff will usually be able to make alternative arrangements for you.

Workshops and labs can present challenges if you have sensory sensitivities. Are any of the following likely to cause you a problem?

- Loud machinery and electric motors

- Wearing protective clothing

- Bright lights, flashing lights

- Sudden bangs or flashes

- Proximity to heat sources, such as Bunsen burners

- Smells from chemicals

- Handling materials of different textures

- Setting up apparatus

- Tasks that require fine dexterity such as soldering

- Dealing with spillages or breakages.

Use the next worksheet to record what the challenges are for you. Share your ideas with your mentor and teacher.

■ SENSORY CHALLENGES

Challenges for me are...

This is because...

> ### Case study: Daniel
>
> Daniel was told that he could not take physics as one of his A-level subjects because he would not be able to do the electronics module which involved soldering. He was upset because it was one of his favourite subjects and he was good at it. A solution was found by arranging for him to have an amanuensis[1] (someone with steady hands to whom he could explain what needed to be done). The ideas were all his own, he just needed help with the 'doing'. The examination board accepted that he needed the amanuensis for his examinations.

Noisy classes

You will remember from school that there were some classes that had students messing about and being noisy. This may still happen at college, even though students have chosen to come to college and chosen their courses. When people start messing about you may feel anxious because the teacher does not seem to be in control and you worry about what may happen next. This may make you feel angry with the teacher and the students and be tempted to shout out, swear or throw things. Other people messing about can be particularly annoying when you are trying to get on with your work.

Use the next worksheet to record what worked for you at school when other students were messing around. Share your ideas with your mentor and teacher.

---

1   An amanuensis refers to someone who can scribe or perform practical tasks for students with fine motor skill difficulties, including individuals with autism spectrum disorder.

■ WHAT WORKED WHEN OTHERS MESSED ABOUT

What worked for me at school was...

Strategies I could try at college...

Negotiate how you might use the strategies in college. Are there any times when you might be a distractor for others? For example, do you rock or hum while you are concentrating on your work? Does it help if the teacher or learning support assistant gives you a non-verbal reminder that you are humming or talking your thoughts through out loud? Does it help to go to a quiet space to work?

No classes, what now?

At school, you had a full timetable with regular break times. At college, your timetable will depend on the subjects that you have chosen. There will be times when you do not have a class but there is no time to go home and get back in time for your next class. We can call this *'fallow time'*, and it is all too easy to waste several hours in a day just waiting around unless you have a plan. No one will tell you how to use the time, which is why you will need a plan for what to do and where to go.

- *What will I do?* Look at your homework diary to see what work needs to be handed in next. Can you complete the work in one of the fallow times or will it need more than one? If there is no homework due, is there an ongoing assignment you can work on? You could also print off your work using the computers available at college. Try to resist the temptation in the IT suite to open up your favourite game, such as *Minecraft* or *Fortnite*, on the computer. There will be time for this out of college hours.

- *Where will I go?* The library or learning support area are good choices if you are going to finish homework or work on an assignment. There may be someone in the learning support area to help you if a task is proving difficult. Or do you need to go to particular places to do that work, such as the IT suite? Look at your timetable for the day and write down when you have fallow time and for how long. Decide where you will go.

Once you have decided what to do during that fallow time and where you need to be, enter it on your timetable for the day. It is now part of your routine for that day.

Help

No one is brilliant at everything, so it makes sense to ask someone for help if you are struggling with a task. It may be that you already help people without thinking too much about it. If you have grandparents, they may have asked you to help them to set up apps on their smartphones or tablets. Family members or even other students may recognize that you are better at some things than they are and ask you for help. How does that make you feel? Most people feel pleased and rather flattered if they can help someone.

On the next worksheet, record how you help other people and how it makes you feel. Share your ideas with your mentor and teacher.

■ HELPING OTHER PEOPLE

I help other people by...

It makes me feel...

You may feel quite comfortable about asking for help to do some things but uncomfortable about asking for help with other things, at home and especially at college. For example, is asking for help with some things ok, for example if you can't find your socks?

Think carefully about when you are comfortable to ask for help. Fill in the following chart by entering each time you asked for help over a three-day period.

■ ASKING FOR HELP

What I asked for help with	Outcome (what happened?)
Day 1	
Day 2	
Day 3	

What makes these situations different from those that make you feel anxious or uncomfortable?

Read the scenarios below. Think about these scenarios and what you would do.

■ ASKING FOR HELP SCENARIOS

You can see in advance that you will need help, for example to move a heavy battery or bench.

- I ask someone for help

- I get angry

- I don't even try

You start something such as moving something heavy and then find that you need help.

- I ask someone for help

- I get angry

- I give up

You do something such as tidy your room and think you have done a good job but are told it is not good enough ('Look, there are still dirty mugs and plates under the bed!')?

- I ask someone for help

- I get angry

- I give up

So far, we have just been thinking about everyday practical problems. Now it is time to think through what might happen at college. We can ask the same set of questions.

You can see in advance that the assignment will be difficult for you to complete on time.

- I ask someone for help

- I get angry

- I don't even try

You start an assignment but it gets confusing.

- I ask someone for help

- I get angry

- I give up

You complete the assignment and hand it in but are told that it is not good enough (there are spelling mistakes and too much detail about one area).

- I ask someone for help

- I get angry

- I give up

There may be many reasons why you might need help in college. Some people have told us what causes them a problem. Some of these may also affect you, but you will have your own ideas too:

- I don't understand the teacher when they explain some things.

- The teacher talks so fast that I don't know what to do when they set a task for class work or homework.

- I can't finish the work in the time allowed.

- I get angry if I have to stop doing a piece of work before I have finished.

- I often get poor marks when I think I have done ok.

On the worksheet below, record what causes you problems at college. Share your ideas with your mentor and teacher.

■ SOURCES OF PROBLEMS AT COLLEGE

What causes me problems at college?

What works best to help you

Some people have shared their ideas, but you will have your own experiences of what works best for you.

1. When the teacher has set a task, I go to the learning support base and talk it through with the teaching assistant (TA) until I am confident that I know what to do. Together we break down the task and write a work schedule. (See Chapter 5.)

2. There is a TA in the room who is there to help anyone who needs it. I put my question mark symbol on my table so that he knows to come to help me.

You will have had good and not so good experiences of receiving help at your school.

Use the worksheet below to record what systems work best for you. Share your ideas with your mentor or tutor.

■ RECEIVING HELP

My ideal form of help is...

This is because...

If you have decided that you will ask for some support, will you ask a:

- family member?

- friend/peer?

- college staff member (support assistant, mentor or teacher)?

The decision about who to ask will depend on what the problem is and your relationship with the possible person you could ask for help.

Think about whether it is a practical problem that is best solved by someone who knows the situation, for example a transport problem may be best supported by the college support team or a timetabling or assignment problem may be best helped by your tutor or the course leader. When you have a problem with how you are feeling generally or when a social situation is going wrong, it is best to go to the person who you trust the most. It can be difficult to find a time to meet with your tutor or course teacher, so it may be a good idea to email them to request a time to meet, giving them a little bit of information so that they have some preparation time to think about the situation. An example of an email requesting a time to meet and basic outline of a problem can be seen below:

> Dear X
>
> I would like to arrange a meeting if possible to talk about the assignment due in on (*date*). I am a bit confused about the requirements and would like some help.
>
> Many thanks,
>
> *name*

Dear X

I would like to arrange a meeting if possible to talk about my group that I have to work with in (*subject*). I am finding it difficult to listen to all their ideas and to get my own ideas heard. I would like some help please.

Many thanks,

name

It can be difficult to talk to other people about personal problems and it may be easier to jot down some key bullet points before your meeting to help you.

Chapter 5

Task and Time Management

———

Sometimes I get in a bit of a muddle with the work and homework so then I just don't bother. (student with autism in first year at further education college)

At college you are expected to work on tasks and assignments in lesson time and at home or in private study times, in what we have called 'fallow' times, when you do not have lessons on your timetable. Some of the strategies that you might use in class are different from those you will need to use in 'fallow' time, or when working at home.

Working in class

Use the next worksheet to answer the questions about what you find hard when the teacher asks the members of the class to do a task.

■ DIFFICULTIES WITH TASK INITIATION

In class, it is hard to:	Yes	No
Motivate yourself if the task has little interest		
Attempt a task which is new or different because you don't know how to begin or you are anxious about getting it wrong		
Know when to apply a skill you have learned in a different lesson		
Show how you worked something out		
Keep the main objective in mind and not get too involved in one part of the task that you find the most interesting		
Complete the task in the time the teacher has set		
Keep calm if you have to stop before you have finished		

If you have answered 'yes' to any of the questions, you may find some of these ideas useful.

Getting motivated

You have chosen the subjects that you do at college, so most things that you found boring or of little interest at school you have left behind. Even so, there will be some topics in every subject that you have chosen that you will find less interesting than others. Unfortunately, these topics are a key component of the course and will have to be tackled. In class, there will be few options but to tackle the task. Think that 'once I get this done, I can move on to something more interesting'. If you do not finish the work in the lesson, you can make some choices about when to finish the work.

The following worksheet will help you make choices about task completion.

■ TASK COMPLETION CHOICES

1. Choose a time: when do you work best – morning, afternoon or evening?

2. Choose a place: do you concentrate best at home or in college? If in college, where is your best place?

3. What will you need in order to complete the task? Will you need access to textbooks, the internet, a printer? *Looking for information on the internet can be frustrating because different sites may hold apparently conflicting views. Look critically at who is providing the information. Look at Chapter 7, Social Media and Computers, for more information about using the internet.*

4. If the task is new to you, will you need help to get started? Your mentor will be able to help you to make the links between what you know already and what you have done before and this new piece of work. It will seem less of a problem once you can put it into a context that is familiar.

Put your plan into the table and stick to it.

Best time	Best place	What I need	Who to ask for support

A new task

It may seem hard to start something that you have never done before, even if the teacher has explained what to do. Feeling stuck? Ask for help.

In class, the teacher will usually set a time limit for the students to complete a task independently. Teachers may say, 'You have 30 minutes to do it.' Let us take an example: Say there are five questions on the worksheet that the teacher may give to you. You have been told you have 30 minutes to do them all. This means each question should take about six minutes. Time yourself for each question.

Each question will be given the same number of marks, so the aim is to spend the same amount of time on each one. You may think you are more interested and know more about one of the questions and it will be tempting to spend most of your time on that question. Remember that the questions will be given equal marks, so if you spend too much time on your favourite topic you may not have time to finish the other questions. You will lose all the marks for them.

Use this worksheet for pace and timing ideas and to practise timing yourself.

■ PACE AND TIMING IDEAS

How long do I have in total for this piece of work?
How many questions or parts to questions?
How much time for each one?

Time myself

Question	Time in minutes
1	
2	
3	
4	

If you have to hand write your answers in class and your writing is slow and hard to read when you try to write quickly, getting the work finished may be a problem for you. Are you quicker at typing? You may already have used a laptop in class at school and for your exams. If so, talk to your mentor about using a laptop in class or being able to take your work to a room where you can use your laptop.

It is useful practice trying to get your work done in a set timescale, because that is what will be expected in examinations. Use the worksheet below to work on speeding up or slowing down.

■ SPEEDING UP OR SLOWING DOWN

1. How long will the task take?   Estimate:

2. How long did the task take?   Time taken:

3. Do I need to work more quickly?   Yes/No

4. If yes, try to beat your time. Did you win?   Yes/No

5. Keep trying to beat your time until you can finish on time

My times ⟶ getting quicker

6. Can I take more time and work more carefully?   Yes/No

7. If yes, slow down and record your times.

My times ———————————————→ getting more careful

However, if you do not finish your class work on time, don't panic. Ask if you can finish the work in your next fallow time. Write when you will do the work on your personal timetable, so that it does not get forgotten or neglected because you have found something more interesting to do.

Stating the obvious

You have worked out an answer. You know that it is correct. Writing down how you came to that answer may seem like an unnecessary chore. However, your teacher does not have access to your brain (fortunately) and does not know how you worked it out or came to that conclusion. It could just have been a lucky guess.

Most questions will ask you to come to a decision based on evidence-based reasoning. For example:

Question: Using the information on the map, find the quickest way from town A to town B. Is it route A, B or C? The map may show diversions, traffic jams and different classes of roads. Marks will be given for your reasons.

Suggested answer: Route A, the motorway, has traffic jams and diversions. Route C has many minor roads and goes through many villages (30mph), so route B would be quickest.

Showing how you got the answer and came to that conclusion is what earns the marks.

There is no 'right' answer

Life would be easy if we could always give one answer to a question. 'Is it raining outside?' will give a clear yes/no response. 'If it's raining, should we call off the trip?' may be harder to answer. It will depend on many different factors such as:

- How heavy is the rain?

- Does the forecast say if it will rain for long?

- Do we have wet weather clothing?

- Will we be outside most of the time?

In the end, it may go to a vote or a judgement call by the person in charge.

The next worksheet contains some questions where the answers depend on context.

■ NO 'RIGHT' ANSWER

What should I pack to take on holiday?
It will depend on... (think of as many ideas as you can, e.g. weather)
What is a good present to buy for a birthday?
It will depend on... (think of as many ideas as you can, e.g. age of person)

As a student, you may expect your teachers to have 'the' answer to your questions, especially in their subject area. However, for some things there may not be a straightforward answer. At the time of writing, no one knows for certain what the impact of climate change might be. We all have different opinions and some people even continue to deny that it is happening at all. Many questions in college and in life will ask you to think about advantages and disadvantages in a specific context, such as building new houses in your neighbourhood.

Practise thinking about advantages and disadvantages using the next worksheet.

■ ADVANTAGES AND DISADVANTAGES

Is the sugar tax a good idea?

Arguments for...	Arguments against...

What is your opinion?
Why do you think that?

People can have very strong and different opinions about things such as Britain leaving the European Union. Only time may tell who is right.

Working independently

In class, the work and how long it will take is usually structured by the teacher. At college, you will also be set longer assignments that may be expected to take days or even weeks. These will need careful planning so that you are not left with too much to do at the last minute. A plan will ensure that you do not get absorbed in the part of the topic that interests you most and neglect the bits that are of less interest.

In Chapter 3, we talked about having zip-up folders for different subjects. You might now need a file for your assignment that has dividers for each of the parts of the topic so that you can keep the notes you make from books or the internet about each part separate.

Looking for information from the internet can become frustrating because different sites may hold apparently conflicting views. Look critically at who is providing the information and decide which is the more credible source. It may be that it is one of those topics for which there is no one answer.

Shorter assignments

Start a plan; for example: Growing coffee in Brazil. The worksheet below has some ideas for your plan.

■ PLANNING SHORTER ASSIGNMENTS

Example: Coffee production in Brazil

Where is coffee grown?

Climate

Soil

Growing cycle

Workforce

Transport to market

Exports

Land ownership

Now go to the internet, your notes from your teacher and textbooks to find out more information about each of the aspects that you will need to cover. Keep the notes in the right parts of your file. When you are taking notes, it may help to highlight key words or use paragraph headings to make sure you get the most important facts. For an example of how to do this, see the worksheet below. Ask your key worker to show you how it is done.

◼ KEY WORDS

The Adolescent brain

Do you want to make some changes in your life? Now may be the time for action.

The brain is a very complicated structure with many different parts that control all aspects of our behaviour: how we move, our emotions, language, memory. Some work done by the brain such as digestion, and our heart beat are largely on automatic control through the autonomic nervous system but for most things that we do we can take conscious control.

Changes take place in the brain during adolescence that may help you with some aspects of your life that you have found difficult up to now. The changes particularly affect the area known as the frontal cortex. This area acts as a control centre for other areas of the brain and is still maturing until we are in our mid twenties.

In adolescence many of the connections between that are not often used and clog up the system are pruned. This leaves us with the most useful connections that can now carry messages more efficiently to all the other areas of the brain. By working on things that you are interested in or want to improve, you can help to shape up this pruning process. For example, you may have had difficulty controlling your temper when things go wrong. Your maturing frontal cortex can help you to stop, think and choose your behavioural options rather than just losing it. The frontal cortex steps in to help you to think about the situation and make a reasoned decision about your best response. This includes weighing up the consequences of what you might do. The process is called self regulation and means that we can make choices about how we respond to situations.

If you are a visual learner, you may find it useful to draw diagrams to illustrate a text.

See the next worksheet for an example of a diagram.

■ DIAGRAM TO SUMMARIZE TEXT

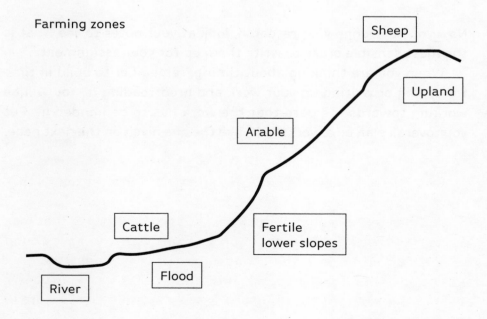

Farming zones

Sheep

Upland

Arable

Cattle

Fertile lower slopes

Flood

River

Mind maps can also help you to organize your thoughts. The following worksheet shows an example of a mind map.

■ EXAMPLE OF MIND MAPPING

Now you have done your research, look at your notes to see what is the most sensible order to write them up for your assignment.

When you are thinking about timing, remember to build in time for typing or writing up your work and proofreading it. You will be working towards the date that the work has to be handed in. Put your overall plan on a worksheet, like the one given on the next page.

■ EXAMPLE OF A MASTER PLAN

Project title: Growing coffee in Brazil

	When (dates)	Where	How long
Research under headings (see 'Planning shorter assignments' worksheet)			
Ordering the headings			
Writing/typing			
Proofreading/ checking			

Deadline for handing in is:

Longer assignments

At college, you will be set longer assignments that may have several weeks as a timescale for competition. Work in class is usually clearly structured by the teacher and the timescale is set for you within the lesson. Longer assignments need careful planning so you are not left with too much to finish at the last minute. There is also a danger that you will spend a lot of time on one section and have little time for the other parts.

Planning
1. Write the title and simplify it to guide what you are expected to do

Example:

> *Question:* There were many consequences of Hitler's invasion of Poland. Outline the causes of this course of action and their effect.

What it means and what you have to write about:

- Why did Hitler invade Poland?

- Describe what happened after Hitler invaded Poland.

- What did the invasion make other countries do?

You may need some help from your mentor to simplify questions at first, until you get used doing it. You will see from this example that there are three parts to the question. Plan to spend the same amount of time on each of the parts.

How long do you think it will take for you to do each part?

2. Practise timing

- Estimate how long the task will take you.

- Write down your estimation.

- Do the task.

- How close were you?

- Repeat this exercise until you can get very close to the desired timing.

Is there anything about the question that is confusing?

Are there any words you do not understand? Look them up or ask someone.

Write down what has happened in the order that it takes place. Sometimes the order of mention is different from the order of action; for example, 'John went back to the house to fetch his tool box. When he went out he had noticed that the fence was broken and the sheep had escaped. The first job was to round up the sheep.'

What is the order of action in this story?

1
2
3
4

3. If you have a text to read that has paragraphs, think of a title for each paragraph

This will help you to summarize the text and identify the main ideas.

In the example about Hitler invading Poland, there were three sections to research.

You will need to find out more under each section heading, using a text or the internet, by writing notes.

Ideas to help with taking notes:

- Key words

- Diagrams to summarize text

- Mind mapping

- Imagery that can help to remember new words and how to spell them.

For example:

Plangent

A suggested outline to structure the plan:

Title
Heading 1
Heading 2
Key points from notes
(Can you use post-it notes for this?)

Once you have a plan and have made your notes, write or type the work. How long will this take?

Leave time for checking and proofreading. This may seem like a chore because you have done the work and it always takes longer than you expect!

The last part of the job is remembering to hand the work in on time, and on the right day. This can be tricky. Some students have found the stacker tray system helpful. Work to be done is put in the stack on the left in the tray marked with the day you need to do the work. Finished work is put in the right-hand stack in the tray marked for the day the work is needed to be handed in.

Use the system shown in Chapter 3.

Chapter 6

Friends and Relationships

▬ ▬ ▬

It's never too late to make friends when you're starting your career in school or college, university or work places. Your friends can help you with work or getting rid of your anxiety. Friendships are very important in your daily life. Relationships can be tough. (student with autism in second year at further education college)

This student reminds us that friends can be very important in our lives and that a fresh start at college gives us the opportunity to meet different people and make new friends. During the course of a day, we will all see many people and may even chat to some of them. Most will be acquaintances rather than friends, but how do we know the difference? Our friends are the people we choose to spend time with, enjoy doing things together and trust to help us out or cheer us up if we are sad.

Use the following worksheet to think about the differences between people we just see often, acquaintances and friends. Where would your online friends fit into the diagram?

■ MY SOCIAL WORLD

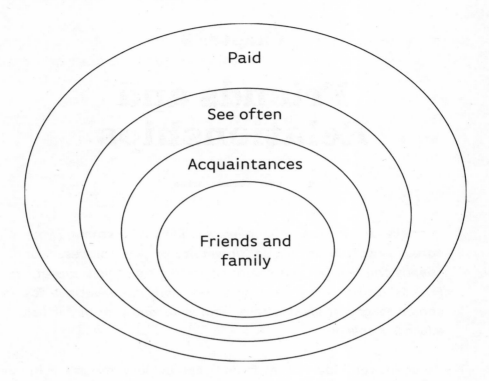

Where would you place cyber friends?

Think about all the people you know. Add them to whichever column below best describes your relationship with them. Think about the differences in how you interact with these different groups of people.

Paid to be in my life	See often	Acquaintance	Friend	Cyber friend
E.g. teacher	E.g. postman	E.g. chat at bus stop		

How can an acquaintance become a friend? Look at the next worksheet.

The second part of the worksheet above asks you to think about how you adapt your behaviour towards those different groups.

The next question to ask is: how does an acquaintance become a friend?

The following worksheet has some ideas about how friendships can grow or, in some cases, not develop beyond acquaintance.

■ FRIENDSHIPS CAN GROW OR NOT

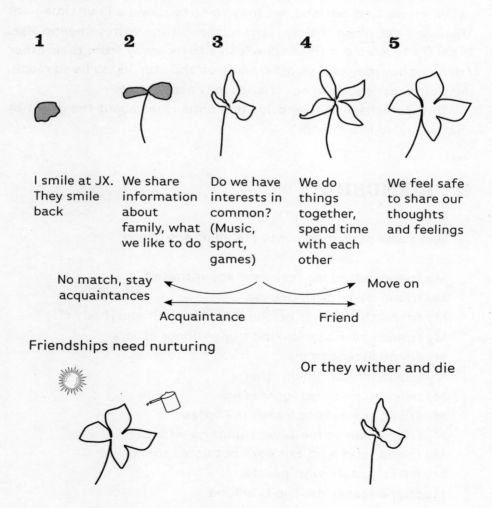

1	2	3	4	5
I smile at JX. They smile back	We share information about family, what we like to do	Do we have interests in common? (Music, sport, games)	We do things together, spend time with each other	We feel safe to share our thoughts and feelings

No match, stay acquaintances   Move on

Acquaintance   Friend

Friendships need nurturing

Or they wither and die

Friendships can be smothered

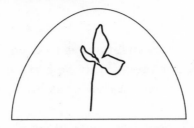

Once we have made friends, those friendships need to be nurtured or they may wither away, as shown above. It is easier to maintain our friendships if we live close by, go to the same college or belong to the same clubs. Once people move away, it is harder to keep in touch, although the internet does make this easier than it was in the past.

When we find a friend, we may want to spend all our time with them and get upset if they want to spend time with someone else. If we try to keep our friends exclusive to us, away from their other friends, they may feel smothered by us and stop liking us so much. Just as plants need air, our friends may need space.

This worksheet on friendship has some ideas about the qualities that we value in a friend.

■ FRIENDSHIP

Sort these statements into friend or not friend:

My friend makes me feel good about myself
My friend never criticizes me
My friend thinks that he/she is better than everybody else
My friend never says unkind things about others
My friend listens to me
My friend makes fun of others
My friend sometimes ignores me
My friend sometimes makes me upset
My friend blames me when things go wrong
My friend talks a lot but does not listen to me
My friend argues with people
My friend teases me and is unkind

My friend expects me to do what he/she wants

My friend takes my things without asking

My friend likes to spend time with me

My friend is moody

My friend always likes to be right

My friend chooses me as a partner

There are those that do describe a friend and others that will make you think whether that person is really a friend. Put them in the following table as Friend or Not friend.

Friend	Not friend

Add to your lists your own ideas about the qualities that you would look for in a friend and those that you would avoid.

Knowing me

Part of being friends with someone is knowing how they are feeling and being sensitive to their needs. In order to read the feelings of other people, we first need to understand our own feelings and how they affect what we say and do.

The next worksheet helps you to think about yourself and how your own feelings affect what you say or do.

■ KNOWING ME

Feeling	What my body feels like	What I do and say
Happy		
Sad		
Angry		
Frightened		
Bored		
Excited		
Anxious		

The next worksheet, 'Me and you', has ideas about people such as how reliable they are. Someone who is reliable will always be there to meet you when they said they will, let you know if they are delayed and finish their part of a joint project on time.

Choose four people that you know, two of whom are family members, and rate yourself against them on the character traits that are listed. Are they more or less like you for each of the character traits? When you have done this, think about what you have learned about yourself.

■ ME AND YOU

Trait	Name:		Name:		Name:		Name:	
	M	L	M	L	M	L	M	L
reliable								
relaxed								
anxious								
brave								
trustworthy								
sociable								
lazy								
careful								
helpful								
happy								

M = more; L = less

Knowing you

Choose a person that you know well. This might be a friend or a member of your family. How can you tell how they are feeling from what they do or say?

Fill in the following chart for a person you know well and then try doing the same for three others.

■ KNOWING YOU

1	Mood	What they say	What they do
	happy		
	bored		
	angry		
	upset		
	excited		

2	Mood	What they say	What they do
	happy		
	bored		
	angry		
	upset		
	excited		

3	Mood	What they say	What they do
	happy		
	bored		
	angry		
	upset		
	excited		

4	Mood	What they say	What they do
	happy		
	bored		
	angry		
	upset		
	excited		

When you have filled in the chart, what can you learn from looking at the similarities between what they say or do according to their mood?

You can put in more practice by watching TV or a video with the sound turned down. Can you guess what the people are feeling? What do you see that gives you the clues?

If you can do this with other people, it is interesting to talk about the clues that you have spotted and those that you might have missed. You might have noticed different clues.

It may now be possible to replay the scene with the sound on to see how accurate you were.

Accommodating to the needs of others

You have chosen some people that you know well and have thought about how you might read the cues about how they are feeling. For each of the people that you chose in the previous worksheet, think about how you behave towards them when you have tuned in to their mood. An obvious one might be if your mum is shouting at your brother – do you keep a low profile?

In the next worksheet, try to match the people you have chosen for the previous worksheet to moods and thoughts about what to do or say.

■ MATCHING TO PEOPLE'S MOODS

For each of the people listed in the 'Knowing you' worksheet, decide what to do or say to match their mood.

Person from 'Knowing you' worksheet	Happy	Bored	Angry	Upset	Excited
1					
2					
3					

4					

Being a friend

We often show friendship by what we do as much as by what we say.

Look at the next worksheet for some examples of a friend in need. What would a friend do in these situations?

■ BEING A FRIEND

What would a friend do?
Linda has forgotten her packed lunch.

Dan has told Mark a secret about being picked for a team. He has sworn not to tell anyone, but all the boys are trying to guess who it might be.

Jane hears some girls criticizing her friend.

James sees a new boy in the corridor looking lost.

Lewis has a new t-shirt. He asks Ahmed if he likes it but Ahmed thinks it is horrible.

Sarah has an accident and is absent from college.

Opportunities to show friendship happen every day.

Next is a friendship log that you can fill in to see if you are taking up your opportunities to show friendship.

■ ACTS OF FRIENDSHIP LOG

Week beginning:	Monday
	Who
	Where
	What I did
Tuesday	**Wednesday**
Who	Who
Where	Where
What I did	What I did
Thursday	**Friday**
Who	Who
Where	Where
What I did	What I did
Saturday	**Sunday**
Who	Who
Where	Where
What I did	What I did

Copyright Kate Ripley (2014)

My public image

Your public image is about how you present yourself to people that you would like to have as a friend and to everyone else in your life. We are all interested in many things and have ideas about issues, from rule breaking to climate change. You create your public image when you make the decision about which of your interests and ideas to talk about when you meet someone new and want to make a good impression.

Here is an example:

My interest	**The group**
Bird watching	Sports club
Playing computer games	Book group
Reading	Environment group
Football	Classmates

Match the interest to the group.

The message is that even if you are a chess champion, you might be advised to talk about the Tour de France or nutrition when you go out with the cycling club.

See the next worksheet to match your interests to the groups that you meet in your daily life.

■ CHOOSE THE BEST TOPIC

People I am with	I will talk about

Chapter 7

Social Media and Computers

——— ——— ———

Social media, such as Twitter, Facebook, Instagram and YouTube, can be useful. However, it can be addictive and distracting for me at college. (student with autism in third year at further education college)

There has been a huge increase in the use of technology, including gaming and social media. As indicated in the quote above, there is a risk of spending too much time using technology for entertainment rather than studying, and this can be a problem when there are 'free times' during your college timetable when you should be studying.

Use the following worksheet to record the amount of time you spent on technology (gaming or social media) in the last week.

■ TIME SPENT ON TECHNOLOGY

Day	Gaming (hours)	Social media (hours)	Total
Monday			
Tuesday			
Wednesday			
Thursday			
Friday			
Saturday			
Sunday			
TOTAL			

Use the next worksheet to identify any times when this could be reduced.

■ REDUCING TIME ON TECHNOLOGY

Day	Total time spent	Possible reduction	New total
Monday			
Tuesday			
Wednesday			
Thursday			
Friday			
Saturday			
Sunday			
TOTAL			

Technology and social media are likely to be used in some form at college to communicate with you regarding your course. Teachers may email you assignments and you will need to send them back. It can sometimes be tricky to think of what to write in an email in these situations.

The following are some example scripts to use to send assignments or to ask for help with assignments.

To send an assignment:

> Dear (*name*),
>
> I am pleased to attach my assignment on (*subject*) which is due on (*due date*). I look forward to receiving your feedback and comments.
>
> Best wishes
>
> (*name*)

To request help for an assignment:

> Dear (*name*),
>
> I am writing with reference to my assignment on (*subject*) which is due on (*due date*). At the current time, I am finding this assignment difficult, particularly with (*details of difficulty*). I would like to request some help and would be available to meet on (*date when next in college*). I look forward to hearing from you.
>
> Best wishes
>
> (*name*)

There will also be other students who will wish to contact you via social media like Instagram, Snapchat or email. It is useful to think of a script to say if you are asked to supply your contact details to a colleague or staff member at college.

Use the next worksheet to consider whether it is a good idea to pass on any details.

■ PASSING ON CONTACT DETAILS

Name of person requesting details	Have you ever met the person?	Are the contact details for a specific purpose?	Is the information being asked for appropriate?
1			
Comments			
2			
Comments			
3			
Comments			

Assistive technology

It may be the case that you used assistive technology in school to support your learning or communication. If you find communicating difficult, there are a range of applications and software available to support you that can be also used in college, including speech-to-text software programs.

The following worksheet will help you identify the applications and software that you have previously used at school and what will help you at college.

■ TECHNOLOGY USED AT SCHOOL

What technology was used at school?

Which of these could be used in college?

Speak to your keyworker or college staff about whether you would find it useful to use any additional assistive technology devices for your course. These may include communication aids, apps or other technological resources to help you with social interactions or to record your work for your college course.

Gaming and social networking sites

Online games and internet chatrooms result in gaining 'friends' but you may not have ever met these people. It is fine to play online games with them if you feel safe to do so, but it is useful to think about the difference between a real friend and a 'cyber' friend.

Use the next worksheet to help you identify the differences between friends and cyber friends.

■ CYBER FRIEND OR REAL FRIEND?

Name	Have you met them in person?	Do you talk together about anything except gaming?	Do you only interact on social media or email?	Friend or cyber friend?
1				
2				
3				
4				
5				

Social networking sites

Here are some social networking sites that may be useful for you:

weareautism.org

https://wrongplanet.net

www.autismspeaks.org

Online safety

If you sometimes have difficulties in working out how social relationships work, then you may be at more risk online. You need to make sure that you remain safe when you are using electronic devices. This means:

- Do not give out any personal information that you don't want to be shared. Perhaps avoid posting a photograph of yourself.

- Make sure you check who is asking for information if you are being requested to give personal information such as your name, address, date of birth or any bank account details. Your bank would not ask for your account numbers or passwords online. If you are unsure, DON'T give out any information, and check with your family or key worker at college what to do.

- Make sure your screen name doesn't include information that makes it easy to identify you, for example your name or your date of birth.

- Restrict who can see your posts on social media, for example keep it to family and friends.

- Remember that once you post something online you can't take it back. Think before you post.

- Be careful if anyone you meet online wants to meet you in person.

- Make sure that if you are suspicious of anyone 'talking' to you online you tell someone at college who you trust.

Use this checklist to ensure you are keeping yourself as safe as possible.

■ KEEPING SAFE ONLINE

	Yes	No
Are you the only person who knows your passwords?		
Do you have different passwords for different social media accounts?		
Do any of your screen names give information about your name or address?		
Do photographs of you posted online include any information that could tell people where you live or your birth date?		
Are you happy with any information you post online being shared with everyone? (Imagine the information being shouted from a large building for people to hear.)		
If someone online asks to meet you, are you sure they are who they say they are?		

Read through the following case studies and decide what the safest thing to do in each case is.

Case studies for staying safe online

> You are scrolling through your emails and see an email which is marked as urgent. You haven't heard of the person sending the email before and it seems to contain a link that it is requesting you to click on. What would you do?

Discuss with your key worker your thoughts about possible actions.

> You meet somebody in a chat room who asks you to send them a photograph and your address and date of birth. They say that they would like to send you some free gifts for being the 1000th visitor to the chat room. What would you do?

Discuss with your key worker your thoughts about possible actions.

> Some friends are part of a group chat and agree to send each other photographs of themselves without clothes on. They say that everyone is going to do it and you must join in to be part of the group. What do you do?

Discuss with your key worker your thoughts about possible actions.

> You are on the internet carrying out some research for an assignment and a link pops up containing some pictures and language that makes you feel uncomfortable. What do you do?

Discuss with your key worker your thoughts about possible actions.

Cyber bullying

Cyber bullying is any form of bullying which is carried out using electronic devices, for example mobile phones, computers or gaming consoles. Cyber bullying is different from other face-to-face forms of bullying because:

- electronic media is available 24/7, constantly

- the audience is much wider

- the bully can hide behind anonymity (they can disguise their identity).

Cyber bullying can be significantly hurtful to people and it is important to keep yourself safe from being a cyber bullying victim or a cyber bully. It may be difficult sometimes to recognize what other people are doing as cyber bullying.

Read the case studies here and decide whether this is cyber bullying or not – and what you need to do if faced with these situations.

Case studies for cyber bullying

You have broken up with your boyfriend/girlfriend after an argument. When you next access your social media account, you find a string of nasty comments about you from people you know at college saying personal things about your body and your looks. Several people have started to join in the conversation and share the posts with others.

Is this cyber bullying? Speak to your key worker about what you would do.

You have broken up with your boyfriend/girlfriend and go onto Ask.fm to talk about how sad you feel. You receive lots of very nasty and abusive comments back telling you to 'drink bleach' and 'kill yourself'. You have never heard of any of the people who are posting these comments.

Is this cyber bullying? Speak to your key worker about what you would do.

Chapter 8

Exams and Anxiety

When I came to college, I told them that I would never do an exam because they scared me too much, but I got extra help at college and exams are not as scary now. I passed my maths and English. (student with autism in second year at further education college)

At times, everyone will feel anxious, experience rejection, and feel misunderstood and downright miserable. Although your feelings are unique to you, they will be shared, in their own way, by all your fellow students. Like them, you too will have times when you feel good about what you are doing and achieving. It is how we deal with the ups and downs of life that is important. This chapter will help you to explore what makes you feel anxious and how you respond when you are anxious and suggest some ideas that will make life feel easier.

You have already started at your new college, so the first focus is on how you are feeling about college life. There may be some places on the campus where you feel comfortable and other spaces that you would rather avoid. In classes, there may be some subjects and tasks that you enjoy but others that you would rather not do. There have been many new people to meet, both staff and students, and some of these encounters will feel more difficult than others.

Now have a go at the following social environment section of the quiz 'Mapping the Landscape of My College'.

The social environment

During the college day we are expected to work with and talk to both adults and other students. Sometimes these social situations can be pleasant but at other times they may cause us anxiety. Some social situations are described below. Mark on the rating scale to show how you feel about them – for example:

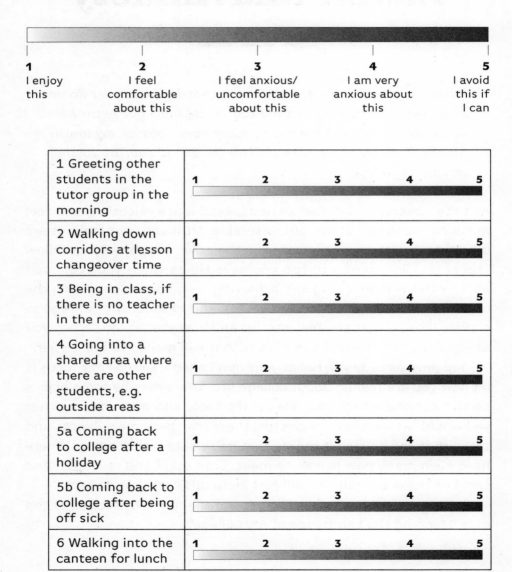

1	**2**	**3**	**4**	**5**
I enjoy this	I feel comfortable about this	I feel anxious/ uncomfortable about this	I am very anxious about this	I avoid this if I can

1 Greeting other students in the tutor group in the morning	1 2 3 4 5
2 Walking down corridors at lesson changeover time	1 2 3 4 5
3 Being in class, if there is no teacher in the room	1 2 3 4 5
4 Going into a shared area where there are other students, e.g. outside areas	1 2 3 4 5
5a Coming back to college after a holiday	1 2 3 4 5
5b Coming back to college after being off sick	1 2 3 4 5
6 Walking into the canteen for lunch	1 2 3 4 5

7 Buying food in the canteen	1	2	3	4	5
8 Sitting in the canteen	1	2	3	4	5
9 Having free time when I have to be around the college with other students	1	2	3	4	5
10 Talking to college staff	1	2	3	4	5
11 Getting to college and home from college: Walk Bus Taxi	1	2	3	4	5
12 Talking to other students in my tutor group	1	2	3	4	5

For the situations that you find most difficult – please write down what would make them easier for you.

What could make a difference...	
Situation	**Idea**

When you have completed this, share the results with your mentor. Discuss what might make the difficult times and places easier to manage.

Now choose a space, a lesson and a social situation where you felt confident and positive. You will have given them a high score (1 or 2) on your forms. Close your eyes, put yourself back in that situation and ask yourself the questions on the following worksheet.

■ FEELING GOOD AND FEELING UNCOMFORTABLE

Feeling good

Knowing me	Place	Lesson	Social situation
What does my body feel like?			
What am I thinking?			
What do I do?			

When you have done that, think of a space, a lesson, a social situation where you felt anxious. They will have low scores (4 and above) on your forms. Close your eyes, put yourself back in that situation and for each one ask the questions again.

There are some ideas that other people have said about how their body feels, the thoughts they have and what they do when they are feeling calm and when they are feeling anxious that may help you to get started, but using your own experiences will help you most. Ask yourself: why does my body feel different when I am anxious and why does my behaviour change?

Feeling uncomfortable

Knowing me	Place	Lesson	Social situation
What does my body feel like?			
What am I thinking?			
What do I do?			

Some ideas

- Physical – relaxed body, shaking hands, sweating, butterflies, heart beating fast.

- Thoughts – happy, worries pop into mind, interested, can't think straight, calm thoughts.

- Behaviour – concentrate well, good appetite, restless, energetic, banging desk.

Humans and other mammals have evolved to respond to danger by a fight, flight and freeze response. A ram meeting a dog may choose to run (flight) or stand and fight. A mouse surprised by a cat may try to play dead (freeze response). These are sensible choices when you feel your life is threatened. In the 21st century, we do not often meet the physically threatening situations that our bodies have evolved to deal with.

However, now imagine that you are out on the sea in a canoe and it starts to sink.

Your body prepares for action in response to the danger:

- Blood is sent to the muscles and brain to give you more power.

- Glucose is released to give energy.

- Breathing and heart rate increase.

- Adrenalin is released.

- Body temperature rises.

All these are responses in our bodies that help us to run faster, think faster, see and hear better and fight harder when we are in immediate danger. Even for the cave man, such life-threatening events did not happen that often, so the body had time to return to its non-alert state for most of daily life. Problems arise for us when we respond to situations, such as going into a noisy, crowded canteen, as if they are real dangers that threaten our lives. Our bodies can go into the fight/flight/freeze mode that is not needed in order to deal with that situation. If we press this emergency button too often, our bodies have no time to return to a resting state and we may get stuck in a state of high arousal that we experience as anxiety or stress.

Use the next worksheet to think about feelings in your body, your thoughts, and what you do on two different days: one when you feel relaxed (A) and the other when you are experiencing anxiety (B). The game is to 'spot the difference' and put your ideas in C.

How confident are you around college?

GET IN TOUCH WITH YOUR BODY

A

At the weekend, Saturday or Sunday, think about how you feel when you first wake up (T1) and pick two other times during the day (T2 and T3).

	How does your body feel?	What thoughts do you have?	What do you do?
T1 wake up			
T2 activity or time			
T3 activity or time			

B

Now choose your least preferred day at college.

	How does your body feel?	What thoughts do you have?	What do you do?
T1 wake up			
T2 activity or time			
T3 activity or time			

C

Spot the difference.

	How does your body feel?	What thoughts do you have?	What do you do?
A most of the time			
B most of the time			

Now rate your confidence using the 'Confident thoughts' worksheet. Share your chart with your mentor and discuss the statements that you have rated as 'not true', then fill in the second part giving examples of your confident thoughts. For example, for 'I can cope with most things', an example may be: 'When they changed the room on the timetable, I stayed calm.'

■ CONFIDENT THOUGHTS

How are you feeling about college? Rate your confidence by ticking the box that is right for you.

Do you agree with these statements?	True	Sometimes true	Sometimes not true	Not true
College feels like a safe place				
I can cope with most things				
Bad things do not happen often				
I can anticipate the bad things that do happen				
I have control over how I react/ respond to things				
People are generally kind and caring				
I feel calm most of the time				
My work is going well				

My examples of confident thoughts

Tracking anxiety in college

You may already have discovered some things that make you feel anxious in college.

The next worksheet will identify what helps you feel relaxed and calm.

■ MY DAILY DIARY

Rate each session from 1 to 10 (1 = most calm and 10 = least calm).

Session	Monday	Tuesday	Wednesday	Thursday	Friday
1					
2					
3					
4					
5					
For the day					

Something good – for each day write down something that made you feel good.

Monday	
Tuesday	
Wednesday	
Thursday	
Friday	

Now set up an electronic diary on your laptop or phone for your college timetable.

- For each session in the day, use a rating scale of 1 = calm and relaxed to 10 = the most stressed ever. There are only five sessions on the worksheet, so you may need to add more. Some days may be different from others, for example if you have work experience days.

- At the end of each day, give that day an overall rating.

- For each day, write down at least one positive experience and one negative. The negative things are the ones that tend to nag at us at the end of the day, so it is very important to counter these with the positive things. Record at least two positives for each negative and focus on the positive ones when you get home.

Looking for patterns

After a few weeks of keeping your diary, you will see patterns emerge and it is time to ask questions. For example, if Thursday is consistently a good day, why is it good and what can I do to make other days more like Thursday?

Fill in the patterns on the worksheet below.

■ LOOKING FOR PATTERNS

Look at the positive things that have happened over the past week.

What are your strengths?
What are your achievements?
What are you good at?
What problems did you overcome? Social   Learning

Ideas to manage stress and anxiety
Deep breathing

We breathe all the time without having to think about it. Here are some more ways of relaxing by concentrating on using our breath. In an exercise class or your own room, you may choose to lie down to carry out breathing exercises, but you can do it anywhere, at any time.

In and out

Take a deep breath while you slowly count to three. Start to breathe out to a slow count of five. Focus on the counting and the breathing to banish worry thoughts. Continue the breathing exercise until you feel calm again.

Horizontal breathing

Put one hand on your tummy and the other on your chest just below your collar bone. Breathe in slowly and deeply. Your tummy should expand and your top hand remains still. Once you have mastered horizontal breathing, try putting a large book on your tummy and taking deep breaths. Repeat 20 times. This will strengthen your core breathing muscles.

4-7-8 exercise

Breathe in for a count of four. Hold your breath for a count of seven. Breathe out for a count of eight.

This is good for relaxation at times of stress.

Muscle relax

The idea here is that you tense and relax each muscle group one at a time. Try starting with your toes – curl them for a count of five, then relax them for a count of five. Now flex your ankles for a count of five and relax them for a count of five. You get the idea? Next move to the calf muscles, thighs, buttocks, stomach muscles and so on, gradually working up the body. This exercise works well if you have trouble dropping off to sleep. Most people never get as far as their shoulders.

Your choice

What do you do to make you feel calm and relaxed? Use the next worksheet to work out whether you prefer physical, soothing or distraction strategies. Then pick two that you could use in college and two that you can use anywhere.

■ WHAT HELPS YOU FEEL CALM AND RELAXED?

Here are some examples of things that people say help them to feel calm and relaxed. As you see some are physical activities, some are soothing and some are ways you might use to distract yourself from what is causing you to feel stressed. Which of the ideas seem best for you? You may not think any of them would work for you.

Which choices do you prefer?

Physical choices	Soothing choices	Distraction choices
Trampoline Cycle ride Play sport	Soak in bath/take a long shower Stroke a pet Snacks	Watch TV or a film Gaming Play an instrument

My calming strategies are:

Physical choices	Soothing choices	Distraction choices
e.g. go for a run	e.g. rock in a chair	e.g. look at YouTube

Which type are you and are you not? (You may have nothing in one of the boxes.)

College choices

Choose two of your strategies you could use in college.

1.
2.

Everyday strategies:

1.
2.

Top tips for self-care

Explore the next worksheet to see how to look after yourself. There are some ideas with a space to put what you will commit to doing: a bit like a New Year's resolution.

■ TOP TIPS FOR SELF-CARE

What can you do to...	I will try to...
Get active, keep fit	
Eat a healthy diet	
Do something you enjoy every day	
Say something positive/good about yourself every day (look at your daily diary)	
Say or do something positive for someone else every day	

Taking control

Learning to think before you act! We all do things that we look back on and think 'Idiot. Why did I do that? I wish I had said/done...instead.' We are more at risk of doing these impulsive things when we feel anxious. Do you remember that in the Introduction we explained how your brain is changing? The part called the frontal cortex is gradually getting better at taking control and stopping you from doing those things that you regret later. You can help the frontal cortex to take control by practising some self-talk about situations that you find tricky.

Look at the next worksheet to think about things that have happened to you before.

■ I CAN MAKE CHOICES

Think of as many choices as you can. Write them down.

1 One choice is:	
Outcome for me	Outcome for others
✓ ✗	✓ ✗

2 One choice is:

Outcome for me   Outcome for others

✔   ✘   ✔   ✘

3 One choice is:

Outcome for me   Outcome for others

✔   ✘   ✔   ✘

4 One choice is:

Outcome for me		Outcome for others	
✔	✘	✔	✘

Select one of your choices. Does it have good outcomes for you and others?

My choice is to:

Write/act out a script. What will you say/do to whom and when?

Practise your script. Rehearse it in your mind too.

Decide when, and with whom, you will test your script.

Evaluate the outcome with a friend/staff member.

Worked well	Try another choice
✔	✘

Set a new target for yourself. When this happens again, I will:

Try the next worksheet to problem solve for a new, different event or situation.

■ PROBLEM SOLVING

Event or situation

My choices are		

Think of as many choices as you can.

1 One choice is:	
Outcome for me	Outcome for others
✓ ✗	✓ ✗

2 One choice is:

Outcome for me

✔   ✘

Outcome for others

✔   ✘

3 One choice is:

Outcome for me

✔   ✘

Outcome for others

✔   ✘

4 One choice is:

Outcome for me		Outcome for others	
✓	✗	✓	✗

Select one of your choices. Does it have good outcomes for you and others?

My choice is to:

Write/act out a script. What will you say/do to whom and when?

Practise your script. Rehearse it in your mind too.

Decide when, and with whom, you will test your script.

Evaluate the outcome with a friend/staff member.

Worked well	Try another choice
✓	✗

Set a new target for yourself. When this happens again, I will:

The next tool is a useful prompt sheet which you can carry round in your bag or pocket, as a reminder to Stop, Think, Do, Evaluate when something unexpected happens.

■ PROMPT SHEET

1. Have I seen this before?

2. What did I do?

3. What can I do differently?

4. Try it out

5. Was it a good choice to make?

Keep this as an alternative to counting to 10.

STOP (red light)

THINK (1 to 4 as script)

DO (carry out my choice)

EVALUATE (5 as script)

Other strategies to try

Imagine a situation when you stayed in control. Picture the scene in detail. Who is there? What are they wearing? Where is it happening? What happened just before? What did you do/say? What did the other person(s) do/say? At the end of each day, record all the situations when you stayed in control. Distract yourself, for example by thinking of a favourite film. Choose a hero. Do you have a super hero, avatar or sports person that you admire? Think like them. What would they do in your situation or if 'this' was happening to them?

Dealing with anger

The next worksheet enables you to list all the things that can make you angry. Some may make you a bit angry and others make you feel wild. They are your triggers.

■ WHAT MAKES YOU ANGRY?

Think of as many triggers that make you angry as you can.

My triggers for getting angry

■ THE ANGER MOUNTAIN

Put your triggers on the place you think they should go on the Anger Mountain.

Now match your list of what you do when you get angry to the triggers on your mountain.

The Anger Mountain

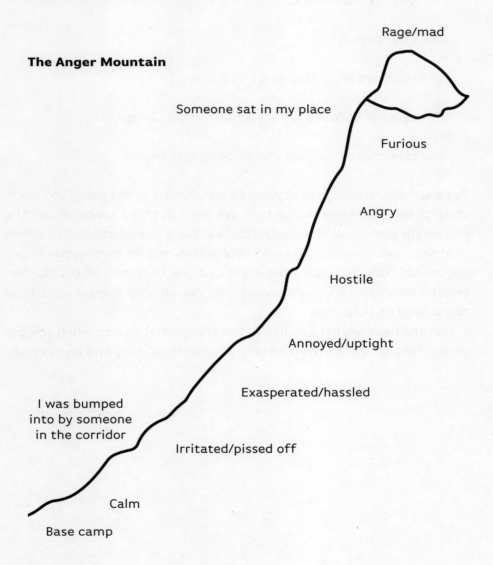

Rage/mad

Someone sat in my place

Furious

Angry

Hostile

Annoyed/uptight

Exasperated/hassled

I was bumped into by someone in the corridor

Irritated/pissed off

Calm

Base camp

Consider these situations and add them to your Anger Mountain:

Computer won't turn on.

Someone copied my work.

I forgot my homework.

I lost my pen.

The teachers were late and I had to wait.

The teacher talked too fast and I couldn't keep up.

The classroom changed and nobody told us.

Put each of the things that you had on your list in the place you think they go on your Anger Mountain. We have put two examples on the mountain already and included beneath it a list of other situations that you can consider and add where they would be on your anger mountain. You may not agree with where they are; if so, change them. The Anger Mountain shows that not all your triggers need the same level of response.

On the next worksheet, list all the things that you do when you get angry. This can range from an angry face to shouting and lashing out.

■ WHAT DO YOU DO WHEN YOU GET ANGRY?

When I am angry, I...

Go back to your Anger Mountain and try to match what you do to the triggers on your mountain. Using the following template, can you make your actions fit the 'crime'?

■ LET THE ACTION FIT THE CRIME

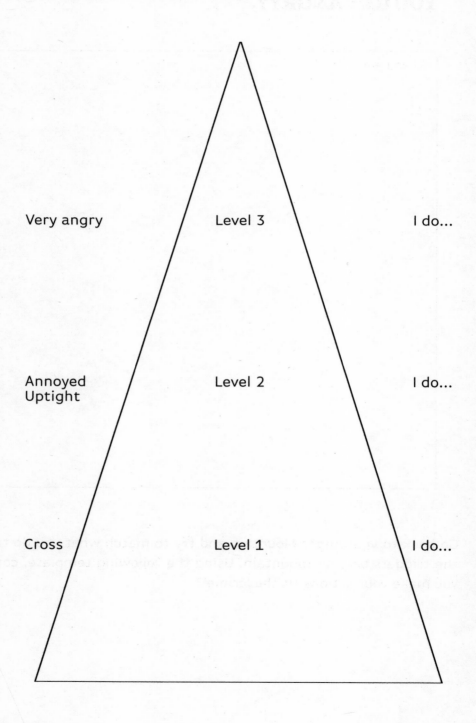

Very angry   Level 3   I do...

Annoyed   Level 2   I do...
Uptight

Cross   Level 1   I do...

Take two things that make you a bit cross (Level 1).

What do you do?

1.

2.

Take two things that make you feel annoyed or uptight (Level 2).

What do you do?

1.

2.

Take two things that make you very angry (Level 3).

What do you do?

1.

2.

Now in the following worksheet list the things you do when you get angry that you will try not to do again. These will usually be things that are likely to get you into big trouble or really upset someone else.

■ I WILL TRY TO STOP

What I do	What are the consequences?
1	
2	
3	
4	
5	

Examinations

You are not alone. Most people freak out about tests and exams. The ideas that you have practised to keep calm and relaxed are those that can help you with exam anxiety too. Here are some extras:

1. *Familiarization.* Ask your mentor to arrange for you to do practice papers in the room where you will be taking the exam and under test conditions. You will gradually get used to the situation and it will feel less daunting.

2. *Can't sleep for worrying?* Take a break from revision at least an hour before you try to sleep. Follow your usual bedtime routine and add in your favourite relaxation strategies. Distract yourself with music or the radio, but remember, no screens. The light spectrum stops the sleep hormone melatonin from becoming active.

3. *Moments before.* Just before an exam starts is peak panic time. Negotiate with your mentor to have a quiet space to wait away from the other students. There you can do your breathing exercises or use your favourite distraction strategies.

4. *The room.* If you find the exam room too noisy and distracting, arrange with your mentor to take the exam in a small space with only a few other students.

5. *Handwriting.* If your writing is slow and if you try to speed up it is hard to read, your mentor can arrange for you to use your laptop or have extra time.

6. *Understanding the questions.* Your tutor will give you practice questions to discuss what is meant by exam speak such as 'compare and contrast'. Practise summary answers with bullet points for what you will include in an answer.

7. *Freeze.* If your hand seizes up and you can't write or type, keep writing/typing your name until you are more relaxed.

8. *Timing.* Equal marks = equal time. You might start with the question you like best and allow just a little more time for that as it may help you to remember and get the thoughts flowing. Otherwise, be a clock watcher.

9. *Banish worry thoughts.* Focus on the task.

10. *If the questions seem hard or are not what you expected,* remember it will be the same for all your class. Pick the question you feel the most confident about to do first. It's not much fun, but what is the worst that can happen? There are always new opportunities and second chances.